Let God be God

Let God be God

GRAHAM LEONARD
IAIN MACKENZIE
PETER TOON

MOREHOUSE PUBLISHING
WILTON, CONNECTICUT

First published in Great Britain by
Darton, Longman and Todd Ltd

First American edition published by
Morehouse Publishing
78 Danbury Road
Wilton, CT 06897

ISBN: 0–8192–1517–1

BT
40
. L46
1989

Printed and bound in Great Britain

Contents

Preface   vii

Acknowledgements   x

Introduction   1

1 Setting the Scene   3

2 Reflecting upon Revelation   8

3 Revelation and Christ   22

4 Distorting Revelation   35

5 Revelation and the Father   45

6 Inclusive Language for Human Beings   60

7 Inclusive Language for God   69

Epilogue   82

Preface

At the heart of the Christian gospel is the belief that God, the Creator and sustainer of the universe, has revealed himself and has redeemed mankind by his actions in history. So in the creeds of the Church we proclaim and thank God for particular events at a particular time – born of the Virgin Mary; suffered under Pontius Pilate; the third day he rose again from the dead. These events in history are the climax of a series of events, beginning with God's call to Abraham and Moses, of which the Old Testament provides the record. They provided the preparation for the unique event in history when the Lord was made flesh and dwelt among us.

The significance of that event has exercised to the full the minds, hearts and bodies of men and women throughout the ages and continues to do so. But the Christian God is not the God who is made in the image of the philosophers, the ascetics, the mystics or the social reformers. They, like all men and women, are brought under the judgment of God who reveals himself by his actions, actions which give the meaning and direction to human history.

It is obvious to anyone reading the Scriptures which provide the record of these events that they took place in a culture very different from that of subsequent ages including the present day. Nowadays it is suggested that in using the Scriptures we must adapt them to suit our culture and our ideas. Likewise it is maintained that we can modify the great images such as Fatherhood, or Sonship, through which God has chosen to reveal himself and which he bids us use in our address to him. Such an attitude runs contrary to the constant affirmation in the Scriptures themselves that the time and place of these events were the result of the deliberate choice of God and effect the working out of his eternal purpose for mankind, created in his own image. As a wise man has said, the purpose of the Scriptures is to enable us to see ourselves – not as other people see us but as God sees us, which is a very different thing.

It was 'when the fullness of time was come, God sent forth his Son, born of a woman' and no mere accident of history. For this reason the time and place of the events of our redemption are not negotiable. To suppose otherwise is to imply that if God had been wiser he would have been incarnate now in our supposedly enlightened times, not in the society of what we now call first-century Palestine.

Certainly we have to discern what is of divine revelation in the record. This our Lord did, in his attitude to the Old Testament, the authority of which he accepted and which in his own Person he fulfilled by obedience. As Maisie Spens wrote, 'The historical events recorded in the Scriptures were never to him mere historical happenings in the past: each yielded to him an eternal and abiding truth and significance upon which he drew in the present circumstances and difficulties of his own life.'* We have to follow his example, not seeking to modify the Scriptures to suit our ideas but to stand under the judgment of those events in the time chosen by God, allowing the Spirit to enable us to hear the Word and obey in our times.

In the first of the Pastoral Letters issued by the Lambeth Conference 1988, it is stated that:

> the meaning of Scripture must be, in fact always is, declared and explained within changing circumstances, cultural settings and language. Scripture must not be made to serve the ends of a particular culture, nor be tied too closely to scholarly trends nor must it be read apart from the particular

---

* In *Concerning Himself*, quoted by Professor R. V. G. Tasker in *The Old Testament and the New Testament*.

experience of people. Discernment is the process through which a body of believers receive the Word of God in its own time and context.

That is well said and it is a matter for sadness that these words are not reflected elsewhere in the recommendations of the Conference, when only too often contemporary culture seems to be the dominant factor.

It is in the spirit of what is said in the Pastoral Letter that we seek in this book to discern in one particular matter, namely that of the language of Scripture, how we can be both obedient to the divine revelation and take account of the proper concern of men and women today.

Acknowledgements

Scriptural quotations are from the Revised Standard Version. The extract on page 57 from T. F. Torrance, *The Mediation of Christ* (Paternoster Press, 1983), is reprinted by permission of Professor Torrance and the publishers; and that on page 70 from Daphne Hampson, 'The challenge of feminism to Christianity', *Theology*, vol. 1xxxviii, no. 725, September 1985, by permission of the editors and publishers.

Introduction

What is our aim?

In brief it is our aim to encourage Christian people to think
Christianly about God's self-revelation and the principles which
govern it; and also to ponder carefully the implications for
Christian teaching, worship and prayer of the adoption of
inclusivist and feminist language both of human beings and of
God, but particularly of God.

Recently we have all been feeling the force of a cultural wind
the aim of which is to remove all traces of generic man from
contemporary English. We are familiar with 'chairperson' or
simply 'chair' for the one who used to be the chairman, and
we shall probably become more familiar with other changes as
the months pass and we move into the 1990s.

In the churches the same wind blows, as evidenced in the
minor changes ministers/priests make in leading worship – for
example changing 'all men' to 'all', and 'fellow men' to 'neighbour'. Further, various reports are beginning to appear (e.g.
Making Women Visible, 1989, from the Church of England's
Liturgical Commission) which seek to control the effects of this
wind. But there are in existence Bibles (e.g. the New English
Bible, 1989) and liturgies (e.g. from the American and New
Zealand Episcopal Churches) which have already sought to
implement the principle of inclusive language with respect to
human beings.

We are concerned that this wind should not blow away, along

with all traces of generic man, the Christian confession of God as our Father, and Jesus Christ as the eternally begotten Son of the Father. We realise that in the Church in which we minister the wind has not yet blown to this extent: but we hear of the beginnings of its effects in cases where clergy and laity tell us that they cannot see anything wrong in praying to God our Mother through Jesus Christ her Child on occasions.

To make our case, we shall invite our readers to think theologically. This means that we try to let the truth of revelation – which is Jesus Christ – speak to us in its own terms as it is found in Holy Scripture and in the creeds. We start from the premise shared by the majority of practising Christians that God has revealed and continues to reveal himself to us in Jesus, the Christ and Lord (by the Holy Spirit) and that the record of, and witness to, this revelation is in sacred Scripture. Further, we gratefully accept the dogmas of the Trinity and the Person of Christ formulated by the ecumenical councils of the Church between AD 325 and 451 as the theological structures by and through which we think of God as the revealer, Lord and Saviour. Thus we see the task of theology not as the construction of theories of what might/could have been, but as obedient attentiveness to the significance of the particular shape and way of God's self-revelation in Jesus, the Christ. So we align ourselves with the method used by such great theologians as Anselm, Barth and von Balthasar.

What we have written is not, of course, exhaustive; but we hope it is suggestive in a positive sense. It is not the kind of popular Christian reading so common today: it is theological, demanding serious and penetrating thinking. We offer no apology; but we urge readers to make an effort, and, where necessary, to re-read a section in order to follow the argument.

1

Setting the Scene

In the first issue of 1989 of *The Times* there was an article on power – the power of the male-dominated Church, exercised to deprive women of their rightful sphere of pastoral ministry. Ronwyn Goodsir Thomas wrote:

> Many feel deeply hurt and excluded by sexist language, seeing the use of exclusively male terms for God as implying that men, rather than women, are made in the image of God, and regarding language which ignores the feminine qualities in God as misrepresenting of God and alienating to women. (*The Times*, 2 January 1989, p. 13)

This is a long and complex sentence. It contains a cry of complaint being made increasingly by women either in, or sympathetic to, the feminist movement. We have no desire to dismiss this cry: rather, we take it very seriously as a sincere call from people who want justice in the Church, and who believe that if what they call for is implemented, the Church will be a more just society of human beings.

The content of the claim

Let us then analyse the cry of complaint. We find that it contains the following claims:

1 The Church uses sexist language in its services of worship.
2 Many (but not all) women in the Church not only feel deeply hurt by this usage but also excluded from authentic

pastoral ministry, which, it is assumed, must include the ordained priesthood.

3 The root cause of this hurt and exclusion is that the Church of which they are members insists on the continuing use of only male terms for God.

4 Women interpret this sole use of male terminology for God as implying that only males are made in the image of God.

5 Another cause of this hurt and exclusion is that the male-dominated language used in and by the Church ignores the feminine qualities of God witnessed to in parts of the Bible and Christian tradition.

6 Thus women are alienated in and by the Church of which they are a part.

We hope that this is a fair analysis of the cry from the heart of Ronwyn Goodsir Thomas.

Our response

We believe that, as male clergy, we ought to take this claim seriously. We ought to submit it to careful examination since a growing number of people hold that it is, or at least appears to be, just.

We sympathise sincerely with those women who feel genuinely hurt, excluded and alienated. We recognise that they believe themselves to be the subjects of discrimination by a male-dominated power structure. We want to confess with them in a clear voice that the Lord our God is not a male deity, and that the view of some of their opponents that he is, is entirely erroneous. Equally we wish to affirm the long-established tradition of orthodox theologians, from the early Church onwards, that God is neither male nor female. We desire to agree with those women, that women have often been badly used and maltreated in our western society: their gifts and talents have not been used for the common good as they ought to have been. We believe that women deserve a better deal in that society.

Further, we accept that to some, the use of what is grammatically known as 'generic man' is irritating, sometimes offensive. Our old liturgies use this device, often in the sense that the term man/men means not 'male person(s)' but 'human being(s)'. It is not our intention to defend this usage as absolutely necessary or binding. We think it has certain advantages in some places, and we shall indicate these later.

However we also have to confess (for the evidence to us is overwhelming and compelling) that this God and Lord, who is neither female nor male in Godhead/eternal being, is revealed to us as Father, Son and Holy Spirit. Try as we may, we cannot see how we can accept God's self-revelation without also accepting that God has chosen to use certain male symbols and male language to express to us the kind of God 'he' is. To cease to use these terms is, to us, to discard that revelation. Yet, what we shall be insisting upon – and we deem this to be most important – is that these symbols and this language are to be understood from within the revelation itself and not from outside (that is, not from the stance and mores of any particular culture). This is the way which God takes in using these as appropriate to point beyond themselves to the incomparable truth which he is. What God intends by Father is what we need to try to understand: and this will be different from the understanding of the term 'father' in any human culture.

Therefore the task we have set ourselves is to consider God's self-revelation and then to bring the cry and complaint of women to the bar of this revelation. First we shall affirm that there is revelation from and of God, that Jesus Christ is its centre, and that in coming from God to humankind, revelation has a method and creates a particular way of thinking and speaking, appropriate to its nature. We shall also explore the biblical witness to the Fatherhood of God.

In the second place we shall invite the reader to consider what we think are cautionary tales. These are the adoption of Arianism by many Christians in the fourth century, and the acceptance by many German-speaking people in the 1930s of a Teutonic Christ. These examples give us clear warning that

revelation can be relativised and distorted by cultural aims
– sometimes well-meaning, sometimes apparently innocuous,
sometimes sinister.

Finally we shall provide examples from the most recent feminist and inclusivist liturgies to show where proposed reforms
are going, and likely to go, if they are allowed to proceed. We
shall analyse their contents to show that the consistent use of
feminine symbols/language projected into God can only lead
us in one direction – into heresy and even into the abandonment
of Christianity. We shall end with a plea to our fellow female
and male Christians to base their faith solely upon revelation
and not to feel the necessity of conforming to the latest (however attractive) fashions of contemporary western culture.

Jesus and women

Before we begin our task, we affirm that we recognise fully
that the attitude of Jesus, our Lord, to women was, in his time
and place, quite revolutionary. Further, we want to state that
we wish to stand by him in his revolutionary attitude and
concern. We are impressed, as we read the gospels, with the
following type of evidence (of which there is plenty):

1 Unlike the rabbis, he had women in the small group who
   accompanied him (Mark 15:40–41).
2 Unlike the rabbis, he spoke with women in public and
   spent time teaching them (John 4:27; Luke 10:39). To teach
   women the Torah was forbidden by Jewish law; but Jesus
   did teach them (Luke 10:38–42).
3 He allowed a prostitute to wash his feet – an act normally
   done by a wife for her husband (Luke 7:36–38).
4 He paid special attention to women and children, and even
   put forward a child as an example (a revolutionary idea) of
   true religion (Mark 10:13–16).
5 He refused to condemn an adulteress – recognising perhaps
   that the law was unjust with respect to women (John 7:53ff).

6 He forbade divorce and insisted that the marriage relationship is that of one flesh (Mark 10:8).
7 He entrusted to women (who were not allowed to be witnesses in courts) the privilege of being the initial witnesses
   to his resurrection (Mark 15:47–16:8).

With St Paul we want to affirm: 'For as many of you as were
baptised into Christ have put on Christ. There is neither Jew
nor Greek, there is neither slave nor free . . . male nor female;
for you are all one in Christ Jesus' (Gal. 3:27–28). And we
want to add that the use by God himself in his self-unveiling
of male symbols and language is entirely consistent with the
attitude of Jesus and the visionary insight of the apostle to the
Gentiles.

2

Reflecting upon Revelation

The way in which most religious people face the question 'Should the Church use inclusive/feminine language about God?' seems to be practical, rather than theological. Certainly they have always been used to praying Our Father and referring to God as 'he': they will find it hard to change such language. However, they are becoming increasingly aware that women are in careers, jobs, positions and places where they were not found even twenty years ago. They may not like the extremists of the feminist movements, but they believe there is justice in the talk of equality and rights for women. They are even prepared to use the word 'sexism' now and again to refer to the attitude of a male-dominated society and Church.

So we accept that, to many, the problem of sexist language in the Church is part of the problem of sexist language in society. If the word chairman has been replaced by 'chairperson' or merely 'chair', they cannot see much harm in the occasional 'O God our Parent' (however awkward it sounds). Further, if the word policeman has now become 'police officer', they cannot see what is wrong in saying 'God's Child Jesus Christ' (again, however odd it sounds). They feel that in the name of justice and fair-mindedness female language for God ought to be given a chance in 'Holy Mother Church'.

Apparently few Christians who are aware of this contemporary western wind of change in language consider the subject from the standpoint of God's self-revelation. That is, they do not ask, 'Has the eternal God of holy love given us a way of thinking and speaking about deity which is valid for all places and all time on this earth?' Rather they assume that the prevailing view that we ought to be fair-minded and use female as well as male nouns and pronouns is right and true – perhaps even inspired by God.

True, there are traditionalists who want to preserve the status quo because they know and love it. They are horrified by changes which they see as tasteless and offensive. Their argument is not theological, but cultural (e.g. literary or aesthetic or another basis). We respect the traditionalist argument in some of its forms, but it is not the position we adopt.

We intend to look at the question of inclusive/feminine language for God on the basis of God's self-uncovering in revelation. Ours is primarily and unashamedly a theological task, for that is where we believe the debate ought to be centred.

All rational people agree that if there is a revelation of and from God, Creator and Judge of humankind and of all creation, then its nature and content must be a primary concern of his creatures. All orthodox Christians believe that God has revealed himself in Jesus Christ and by the Holy Spirit, and is engaged in the disclosing, unveiling and uncovering of that self-revelation, once-for-all-time made in Christ, in order that we, whatever our time or place in creation, may truly know, trust, love, worship and obey our God. However we need to discuss together, and hopefully agree on at least three areas: first the method of revelation – the way God takes in disclosing himself; secondly the type of thinking required in us – so that we may be recipients of revelation; and thirdly the nature of the truth of revelation – its essential content.

The case that we shall make both against the adoption of inclusivist and feminist language for God, and against the idea that male terminology carries maleness into God, is a theological one, and is based on the unavoidable implications of revelation from and of the Creator to the creation. This is why we ask our readers to ponder very carefully the issues we shall raise in this chapter; and to do so even if they feel that our treatment and discussion is inadequate in some way.

The method of revelation

There appear to be three possibilities for explaining the claim
that God disclosed himself to Israel and in and through Jesus
Christ. One is to say that revelation always transcends the
environment and circumstances of this world of time and things,
but never becomes a part of it. According to this approach
God makes his will known to his creatures without being
involved with them in their time and their place except, as it
were, at arm's length. It is as though he is outside a room but
never goes inside it himself. We reject this account. God is not
a prisoner of his own eternity. He is free towards his creation.

Another possibility is to claim that revelation is God's touch-
ing of a few minds, so that from them comes forth great insight,
wisdom and knowledge. God, as the immanent Spirit within
the created order, inspires some human beings so that they
become the inspiration to the rest in matters of belief, morality
and spirituality. We reject this account also. Revelation
becomes then a matter of first and second class.

The third possibility, which we favour because we believe it
is in harmony with the content of Scripture, may be expressed
in this way. God in self-revelation enters and masters the
environment from within it, with respect to its creaturely
dimension, in such a way as to transform it, thereby making it
his chosen means of disclosing himself, his Word and his will.
This method can be illustrated best by considering the experience of Jacob as he wrestled with the messenger from God –
identical with God (Gen. 32:24ff).

Jacob faced the wrath of Esau, his brother, and did not know
what to do to escape. He could only look to the God of his
fathers to save him. He struggled with God's messenger at
Peniel. The conflict proved to be both a defeat and a victory
for Jacob. He was crippled in the struggle, but given the new
name of Israel. His limp would be the lasting reminder of
that wrestling, while the new name would ever reflect his new
relationship with the God of his fathers (his new name means
'God contends' or 'God rules'). So God mastered him without

destroying him, and established him in his true identity in his new relation with God. Jacob's will to succeed remained, but he was purged of self-sufficiency and pride, and made to trust the Lord God in humility. God's mastering of him was necessary if he was to become the covenant partner with God and give his new name to the people which would become his descendants.

The principle of mastering in order to transform is seen throughout the Old Testament. For example the Torah (the Five Books of Moses) shows how God transformed various laws, customs, ceremonies and rituals which are known to have existed in the cultures/religions of the peoples around Israel, by bringing them together for a new purpose in the covenant conditions and existence he gave to Israel. God, we may say, through Moses, took over much that already existed and by his grace transformed it by setting it in a new context. Then, when the Torah existed, priest and prophet and king applied the contents to the people to whom they ministered so that the people should fulfil the covenant and be a holy people – 'Be holy as I am holy', God had said to them. Thus the process of transformation was to go on from generation to generation.

The greatest example of this principle (to which all these previous Old Testament examples pointed, and in which they were gathered up and fulfilled) is seen in the incarnation of the eternal Son of God. Here we are astounded to observe that the mastering of all creation was achieved through the form of lowly service, suffering and sacrificial death. The apostle Paul confesses this truth in his poetic section in Philippians 2:6–11, where he describes the One, who always has the very nature of God, becoming man, living a life of obedience to God which involved the cruel death of the cross. Here divine mastery is achieved by way of the suffering Servant, who, on completing his vocation, is exalted by God to the position where all will finally recognise him as Christ the Lord and glorify God in him. In Jesus God masters human nature and overcomes sin and death, so that in his resurrection body of glory he is exalted to heaven, from where he pours out his Spirit on those who

call upon him and assemble in his name. Thus the process of
mastering and transforming continues as individuals are united
to Christ and each other in the Body of Christ, where they find
their true identity, the new humanity, the new creation, as the
Holy Spirit does the work of Christ in every time and in every
place.

God's self-revelation is not given to us merely for our consideration, reflection and meditation; God reveals himself to
us in order to make us his loving, trusting and obedient children
as he masters our pride and self-sufficiency and transforms
them into humility and trust in his name. The Blessed Virgin
Mary stands as the vanguard of all who are overwhelmed by
the loving grace of God – 'Behold the handmaid of the Lord;
so be it unto me according to thy word'. St John of Damascus
was one of the early theologians (though there were others
before him) who (rather quaintly to us, perhaps) pointed out
that the organ of conception was the ear of the Virgin. She
heard the Word of God and obeyed, subjecting herself. And
in our hearing and obeying in the power of the Spirit, a little
incarnation of the truth occurs in us, and with a labouring and
travailing in the Word, the fruit of godliness is brought forth.

The 'mystery of Godliness' (1 Tim. 3:16), God manifested
in the flesh, is the ground of our godliness in him. Only by our
union with the incarnate Lord can we possibly become holy.
For certainly God intends to make us holy – for to that end
were we created – and to do so according to the truth which is
Jesus, the Christ and Lord, applied to us through the presence
and action of the Holy Spirit. Revelation and reconciliation
belong together and cannot be prised apart. God reveals himself to us in order to bring us into a right relationship with him
– and fulfil the purpose and destiny for which humanity was
created.

Accepting this general method of revelation then, we commit
ourselves to certain consequences. For example, since God has
mastered the environment, we are committed to use only those
concepts, images and symbols of him and his will which are
contained in the record of revelation, or such as are in harmony

with scriptural usage. Further, and to this subject we now turn, we are committed to giving priority to a particular way of thinking which is required in order to be recipients of revelation, and which is formed by that revelation itself.

Right thinking

To make clear the nature and content of the type of thinking required in order to receive revelation, and formed by that revelation, we shall first describe two other types of thinking. Both are common to our culture and often intrude into the way we think about God in his self-revelation. In setting out these two we should try to ponder how unconsciously and commonly they have become part of our mental make-up and our day by day attitudes to so many things and circumstances.

There is that way of thinking which is in fact associated with ancient Greece (on the philosophy and culture of which much of our present pattern and modes of society historically rest). The ancient Greeks were interested in the form of things, and not in their substance, which was regarded as part of this passing and decaying world. They believed that in the perfect form of an object, the truth about that object was to be found. They arrived at idealistic theories about things out of surface inspection of them, and into that theory they were made to fit. That is why their architecture was a quest for the perfect form, and their statues idealised and stylised figures. Theirs was a visual and formal way of thinking. But in so doing, they made a great gulf between form and content, between what things appeared to be and what these things really were in themselves. The limitation of this was that the knowledge of things was based only on what was seen of them. But appearance and reality are not necessarily the same. The form of a thing does not clearly or necessarily reveal its true content, whereas the true content of a thing tells more about the form than can be seen on the surface.

This way of thought may be described simply as 'thinking by

seeing'. To a great extent we have inherited this tendency. It would be a most difficult exercise to try to stop ourselves using words of seeing or looking or observing in describing what we think is the truth of things or events or circumstances, for we use them so habitually. Do we not often say in everyday usage 'Do you see that?' or 'Is that clear?', meaning 'Do you understand that?' 'Seeing is believing' is a common enough attitude. The word 'evidence' used as 'the truth of the matter', is a 'seeing' word. Much of the time it is true that things are as they appear to be. We see an aeroplane in the sky and, sure enough, there is an aeroplane in the sky. However in such comments as 'Beauty is only skin deep' or 'Do not judge a book by its batters' we recognise (another 'seeing' word in our usage of it) the shortcomings of this view (yet another 'seeing' word) that 'seeing is believing'.

In the second place there is an eminently practical way of thinking which we associate with ancient Rome and its empire – straight roads, structured laws and effective administration and government. These were all the products of Roman practical application and achievement. This outlook, which is basically regarding things as to the profitable use to which they can be put, and the ways in which they can be made to accomplish this, has left its mark on many of our attitudes and institutions. The technological mind is ever opening up new areas where things can be practically applied and manipulated. The place we accord to technology and its remarkable achievements, and the faith we put in its apparently endless possibilities for promoting standards of living, is all part of this way of thinking. We think about nature, things and even human beings in a practical way, in order to work out how we can best use it/them for whatever practical ends we happen to hold as important.

An illustration of this way of thinking and working may be taken from the attitudes prevalent in the 1960s. Among the many problems which arose for society the question of housing was one of the most pressing. The constituent parts of that problem were: the need to house a growing number of people dependent on local authority housing departments; the cost of building; the prohibitive expense of buying land. These were pragmatically resolved. Land is dear, therefore only small areas can be purchased; a great number of people have to be housed; therefore build upwards in a prefabricated construction, saving space and cost. The result was the high-rise block. There soon became apparent all the psychological traumas associated with the way of life in such housing – the high-rise syndrome. The problem had been looked at theoretically and practically in terms only of technology and finance, and of treating people as statistics. What was not taken into consideration was the sort of creature human beings are – that they cannot be forced to fit into a convenient technological plan which answers only surface considerations and questions. The quality and need of human existence is not something that can be truly and essentially perceived by mere surface inspection and resulting theory.

A supposed knowledge of humankind, based only on observation and erected into a framework of social theory (or any other comparable ideal), when imposed upon human existence can threaten genuine human being and dignity. For example if the individual is seen only as a unit of potential productivity, then the individual's worth must inevitably be seen only in economic terms. Certain things concerning the human spirit are counted as of no moment or even absurdly useless, so devaluing or discarding much of what is essential to the fullness of human existence. Man the maker, or technological man, alone is all in all.

The combination of the Greek and the Roman elements in our thinking has led to a strong tendency within our culture to suppose that we can only know what we can observe and control. This includes not only natural objects, but is held to include humanity as well. What does not fit neatly into these categories is usually relegated to the unimportant or the meaningless. So it is not surprising that within our western society there is little readiness to think about revelation, for to do so, we shall now suggest, requires a different way of thinking. Also it is not surprising that when people think about revelation in the categories we have just described, then they will be unlikely to understand it on its own terms, for they will (unwittingly) fit it into the system of thought which they have already arrived at, and which they bring to bear upon it – a system which decides what is and what is not true.

Happily there is a third formative strand which lies behind our modern way of thinking and speaking. It has been to the fore within the scientific community at those times when natural science has made great leaps forward in new discoveries. It is perhaps best summed up in the advice given by Einstein when he spoke of the necessary 'awe and humility' which one has to have before the self-disclosure of created realities in all their awe and wonder, realities which challenge us at every level of existence. It is the Hebrew (biblical) way of thought and is best characterised by 'listening and making answer, obeying and serving'. We may claim that the history of Israel, recorded in the Old Testament, is the epic of a people confronted with the living God, and how that people stood before this God as he disclosed himself to them. Thus Israel was a parable (meaning 'an astonishment, a by-word, a stumbling-block') held up as a mirror to all the nations. For in Israel was reflected how it was to stand as created humans in such proximity to the living Creator of all. In that mirror, dark and enigmatic to all human standards and ideals, God and what God required was seen. The 'Hear, O Israel' resounding throughout the Old Testament is the uncovering of the sort of God that God is, and how humanity, his chief handiwork, the 'crown of creation', stands in that light. It speaks of a God who acts in a manner consistent with his nature. He is as he acts and acts as he is. There is no contradiction between his being and his acts. Moreover he is the God who personally involves himself in his acts.

The God of Israel was and is the God who took and takes the initiative, the God who actually revealed himself. He was not a hide-and-seek God who required to be discovered by human enquiry or ritual, but a loving and revealing God, uncovering himself in his deeds, relationships and word. Yet the Old Testament is not only about the uncovering of God. It is also concerned with the uncovering of the human ear to hear the things of God. In the Old Testament we see the mental tools being hammered out whereby humanity is enabled to think properly concerning the being and nature of the God who so reveals himself. This uncovering of the human ear and this preparing of the human mind required disciplined listening (to the exclusion of all other claims) as well as the appropriate obedient response to what was heard (to the forsaking of all other demands and alluring thoughts).

This is an objective way of thinking. The mind is directed to the object revealing itself, and in this process it allows the object to 'speak' on its own terms and disclose itself to be what it really is in itself. It excludes the intrusion of our presuppositions about what that object is or should be; and it prohibits our forcing that object into a framework of our own devising. Thus it requires intellectual 'repentance' and 'humility' as reality and truth are disclosed to us. Indeed it requires intellectual reform, as in the light of what we learn more and more from the self-disclosing object we are compelled to revise our previous opinions and beliefs about it again and again. Such thinking produced what may be called the biblical mind, and is, as already noted, fundamental to the progress of true science.

We are convinced that those who seek to think in this way will find it impossible to admit the possibility of any other descriptions of God than those which arise from the biblical witness to him, which relates both to the order of creation and to that of redemption. For this way of thinking sets out our relationship to what is truth.

Reflections upon the nature of truth

We wish to make three observations about the nature of that truth, and then three further ones in the light of the first three, on our relationship as thinking beings to that truth. We recognise that, to follow these, great concentration of mind is necessary. We believe that our readers will find – in the longer if not the shorter term – that these observations help to clarify

the general questions which are fundamental to what we are
trying to say:

God is what he reveals himself to be
This truth is that which cannot be other than what it really is.
It is absolutely consistent with itself. This is its inner integrity.
It also discloses itself to be what it is. It reveals itself to be
exactly what it is. This is its outer integrity. It confronts us in
all the indisputable integrity, freedom and authority of what it
actually is, and by that very fact compels us to assent to it and
acknowledge it to be what it is. Thus God in his self-revelation
is towards us – without any diminution, change or deception –
what he is eternally in himself. What he is eternally in himself
is what he is in his self-revelation to us. There is no disjunction,
gulf or contradiction between what God is, and what he is in
his revelation to us.

*What God reveals of himself is the truth of what he is – not
what human imagination has created*
We cannot invent, discover or master God by our own natural
efforts. Any concept of deity or God arrived at through human
enquiry and effort alone is merely the divinisation of our subjec-
tive state – our self-opinions. To know God we must be encountered by God himself. In revelation we are confronted with
God's self-evidence; he can be the 'hidden God' coming out of
his secrecy as the 'revealed God'. We come to know him in his
own being – what he actually and really is – for he is personally
involved in his self-revelation to us. It is through his Word and
Spirit that we know him. They are God, not something about
God or something of God. It is the very being of God which
causes us to know him, and therefore the being of God and
the truth of God are revealed to us. The very being of God
and therefore the very truth of God confront us objectively in
his self-giving. In revelation there can be no notion that God
must fit our conception of what truth is.

God accommodates himself to our limitations, but does not compromise his being
This truth of the eternal God is revealed to us within the limitations of our capacities, and with respect to these. For in and by his Word and Spirit, he accommodates himself to these. In so doing he does not suspend our creaturehood or scorn this limited world of time and things. He opens out our human and finite limitations to himself as our Creator and Redeemer. Moreover he remains faithfully himself – he does not change, diminish or compromise his being – and therefore the integrity of his truth confronts us within our limitations. We know him, even in and with our limitations in this world of time and things, as the God he is; that is, the God he is in his eternal and limitless existence. The creature is given and made aware of a proper relationship to the Creator, and thereby is established in its true creaturehood, made in the image of God.

The next three observations are:

Human words cannot imprison God
We need to make a distinction between truth and truthfulness. For while God gives himself to be known in the truth of what he eternally is, he does not surrender himself to us to be mastered by us. He gives himself, but does not give himself up. That is, he does not succumb to the mastery of our minds and their limitations. Rather he still remains Lord over our minds; but in the exercise of his loving Lordship he allows our minds to be opened to what he is in his self-revelation. Truthfulness is therefore openness to the truth: and the truthful mind of right reasoning is that mind which is orientated in accordance with the nature of the truth. However the truth maintains and retains the priority and lordship of its being, for it is what it is before and after it is recognised by us. Whatever we think, it remains the truth. It is not changed in what it essentially is in itself by any misrepresentation of it by us. In fact it is, in itself, that which causes our perceiving of it, compels our obedient receiving of it and remains the totally

sufficient and only source of our conceiving it. Truth is above truthfulness, for only truth can uphold our truthfulness towards and concerning it.

Statements about the truth are only approximations

We need to make a distinction between truth of being and truth of statement – that is, the truth which an object really and essentially is in itself, and the truth of what we perceive and say about it. It would be irrational to suppose that an artist could capture the actual reality of what a landscape really is, that is, actually convey that landscape as it exists, on canvas. But his art is a representation of what he cannot convey in the totality of what it actually is. This points the mind to an appreciation of the truth, or an aspect of it. So it is with verbal statements about truth. Truth can never be wholly reduced into a statement about truth. Statements about truth must always be subjected to the compulsion of objective truth itself, and referred to that truth again and again for testing and revision as to their truthfulness. That is why there is a constant need to reform and refine theological statements. When a statement about truth is in accordance with the nature of that truth as it reveals itself in all its majesty, freedom, authority and integrity, then that statement is used by the truth to display more and more of what that truth actually and essentially is in itself, and what itself can only be. The Church has held that the statements about Jesus Christ and his relationship to God the Father in the Nicene Creed are of this kind. They point beyond themselves to what the limitless and inexpressible majesty of the truth is. Truth of being remains sovereign over truth of statements (even credal ones) about it. They are relativised by the truth, not the truth by them.

Authority belongs to the truth, not to statements about it

We must acknowledge that our statements about truth, and therefore our minds and reasons which produce these state-ments, always fall short of truth and are under its judgment. This acknowledgement is an essential element in the continued propriety and truthfulness of our statements about the truth. Further, it means that we must recognise that we do not, indeed cannot, posit any authority or criterion of judgment concerning the truth but the truth itself in all its sufficiency and integrity. Truth is only known on the ground of its own authority. When we say 'an authoritative statement concerning the truth', the authority in fact reposes in the truth and not in the statement as such. The authority of the statement is only deemed to be such in so far as it is appropriate and obedient to the nature of the objective truth. It is authority at second-hand, and is valid only as it serves the truth. It follows that no other concern – however high and laudable or apparently self-evident or universally valid – must be allowed to intrude into the domain of truth. Such intrusions become the authority and tend to confuse themselves with the truth by colouring or distorting the mind's perception of the truth, and the reason's obedience to the truth. They turn the truth into statements about it on their own terms, for they have become lord over it. It is precisely this which lay behind the fourth-century Arian heresy (see ch. 4) and its method of dealing with the truth of God. It was this false teaching which Nicene theology attacked.

Conclusion

We must beware of a false relativity. Our reason is relative to the truth in its self-disclosing, intrinsic freedom and majesty of integrity. There is a necessary contingency of theology, but there is no contingency of the truth. It is sufficient in, for, by, with and through itself. Revelation cannot be relativised for it is not dependent upon our reason, cultural expressions and prevailing opinions. It speaks out to these, but not from them. It alone is autonomous, and all else is judged by it. To relativise revelation into the mould of human inventiveness is to make an idol of the human mind and reason.

3

Revelation and Christ

In this chapter we shall begin our reflection upon the theme of God's self-unveiling and self-revelation from words in the Nicene Creed: 'And was incarnate by the Holy Ghost of the Virgin Mary, And was made man'.

First we note that he who was incarnate is described as 'the only-begotten Son of God, Begotten of his Father before all worlds' (that is, eternally), 'God of God, Light of Light, Very God of very God, Begotten, not made, Being of one substance with the Father'. The eternal Son of God took to himself flesh in the womb of the Virgin Mary: and without ceasing to be God, without discarding or changing or compromising his God-ness in any way, he became man. The fact of the virginal conception (through the creative action of the Holy Spirit) testifies to the truth that he who was born of Mary was not, with regard to his divinity, a new Person. In the way of nature, the conception of a child means the creation of a new person. But the Person of the eternal Son of God took to himself human nature taken from Mary the Virgin. He exists eternally as God, but from a given point in time he has existed with a human nature.

It is not that there existed a man called Jesus whom the eternal Son of God decided to associate, adopt and take into union with himself. The human being of Jesus only has exist-ence, from the moment of conception, in union with the divine being of the eternal Son. There is no humanity of Jesus which existed independently outside this union, with an identity of its own. But within that union there is a real identity and existence of the humanity of Jesus. The historical Jesus is the Word made flesh, and no other.

That is what is new. St Athanasius, in the fourth century, pointed to the astonishing fact that this is a new beginning for God, who exists as God in God, but now also exists as God with human flesh and nature. Therefore we say Jesus is the Son of God.

In the second place we observe that the Greek word *enanthropesanta* which is translated 'was made man' in the official texts of the Creed, can also be translated 'and became human'. This reminds us that the word 'man' in the official text is being used in the generic sense. The Son of God became a human being, bone of our bone and flesh of our flesh. And this of course is what incarnation means: 'The Word became flesh and dwelt among us.' He did not take an angelic nature and body, but took our human nature, which, we recall, is created in the image and after the likeness of God.

The Son of God therefore became what the old theologians have called universal man. The Greek phrase used was *ho kuriakos anthropos* – lordly or dominical man. Because the One by whom all things were created, and for whom they were created and in whom all things consist, took human nature to himself and was born Jesus, all humanity (and indeed all creation) is fundamentally related to him in a way in which its very being is involved. The theologians of the early Church also spoke of all things being summed up – gathered up into a head – in Jesus Christ. This they called recapitulation. All time and things and all humanity is radically touched, grasped by what the Word made flesh is and does. All things and all time are poured into the crucible of what he is and does in his incarnation, death, resurrection and ascension, and are re-created. The new heavens and the new earth, the new humanity and our real identity as individuals, are already present in Christ, though not yet openly disclosed.

At the same time we must also speak of the Son of God incarnate as a particular man. Being born of the Virgin Mary, he was given a name, Jesus, and he lived in a specific family in certain places at a given time. As the Creed declares: '(He) was crucified also for us under Pontius Pilate. He suffered and was buried'. He suffered, died and rose from death as a particular man, Jesus the Christ, but what he achieved 'for us and for our salvation', was because he was also universal man. We must note also that he was a particular man, for the reason that the Word did not become some principle or theory of humanity. Indeed we must point out that the Word became specifically Jewish flesh, in all the realities of a given time and place, and not some theoretical generalised cosmopolitan humanity. Certainly he did so for all humanity. But the only way that humanity is really and tangibly expressed is in the individual.

The Son of God took flesh to himself. That means that he took the wholeness – body and mind – of human nature to himself. But it also means human nature under the judgment of God, where human nature is seen questionable before the holiness of God and in abject need in its rejection of God and his righteousness. God takes, in his unbounded and faithful love, the lost cause of his creature upon himself, to bring the creature into a right relationship and a godly existence with himself. That is the profundity of the incarnation. The re-creative reality of God in his Son is brought to bear on the reality of our human estate, and the work of re-creation is done from within, with loving respect to creaturehood. And this creaturehood is only expressed in all the particular tangibility of individuality.

Perhaps one mistake so generally made is to place the universal aspect solely on the humanity of our Lord, again as though it were a general principle in and by itself, and not see that its universality lies in its relation to the eternal Son of God who took it into union with himself at the incarnation. This is to wrench the humanity of Jesus from its proper place and time, matrix and reality, and to mould it to fit into our theories of universal humankind and what that should be.

We should always hold together and respect these two aspects, the universal and the particular, of the one Son of God incarnate, in our theology and worship. Yet at times we must concentrate on one aspect (without, of course, discarding the other) in order to gain clarity of mind concerning it. Here we intend to reflect upon the particularity of Jesus, for this has strategic bearing upon the general topic we are considering. We wish to affirm that he was a Jew of Palestine, speaking Aramaic/Hebrew (and perhaps Greek), dressing as a travelling rabbi, and having relatives. Then, having done this, we shall proceed to consider the terms Father and Son as being the very words Jesus used and sanctioned.

The particularity of Jesus Christ

The incarnation did not happen at any time: it was in the 'fullness of time' that God sent forth his eternal Son. The incarnation did not occur in any context: the eternal Son of God was born of Mary 'under the law', the Jewish law (Gal. 4:4). There is a definite programme set out by God as the context of this stupendous event.

God's choice of Israel – a race that was nothing in the eyes of the mighty empires and magnificent cultures around – sets the tone of this programme. The story is told of Hilaire Belloc at a City of London dinner: when the then Lord Mayor (a Jew) was speaking, Belloc wrote on the back of his menu card, 'How odd of God to choose the Jews', and passed it to his neighbour. The latter wrote in reply, 'How odd, Hilaire, that you should dare to doubt and prod the choice of God!'

The choice of Israel cannot be ignored, altered or nullified: attempts to do this must ultimately fail. In fact the choice of God of this – and not another – people points directly to God's favoured mode of action, and therefore to the sort of God he is. It is a work of grace, free and unmerited, as the Old Testament itself points out, and not a reward for cultural achievement or proud might. God chooses that which is insignificant and small in the eyes of human standards, and works with it, in order that the sheer overflowing of his unsought-for love might be seen in all its fullness.

He chose Moses, the great law-giver, out of a cradle of rushes; Samuel, the valiant prophet, from a servant's pallet; David, the foremost king, from the sheepfold; and, in the fullness of time, the One by whom all things were created, from a stable in Bethlehem, a poor sorry village scarcely worth a mention in the epic of nations. The eternal Word, whose realm is God's glory, lies in a rough manger, unable to utter a word.

One of the fathers of the early Church, St Irenaeus, writing in the second century, highlights this deliberate plan of God to prepare for and move towards the incarnation in the background of the history of Israel. He writes of the eternal Word of God moving in that history towards his incarnation:

[He was] Patriarch among the patriarchs; Law in the laws; Chief Priest among priests; Ruler among kings; the Prophet among prophets; the Angel among angels; the Man among men; Son in the Father; God in God; King to all eternity. For it is he who sailed in the ark with Noah, and guided Abraham; who was bound along with Isaac, and was a Wanderer with Jacob; the Shepherd of those who are saved, and the Bridegroom of the Church; the Chief also of the cherubim, the Prince of the angelic powers; God of God; Son of the Father; Jesus Christ; King for ever and ever. Amen. (Fragment 53, cf. also 54)

By this background recorded in the Old Testament God taught, piece by piece and part by part, the significance of the great issues of life and death, light and darkness, truth and error. By the lamentations and rejoicings of psalmists, the exhortations of prophets, the example of wise kings, the blood of temple sacrifices offered by priests, the experience of Exile and Exodus, Israel was brought face to face with the righteousness of God. No race has ever experienced such intensity in the contradiction between God and humanity, and no people has ever known such cost in resolving that contradiction.

We must therefore make the Old Testament our schoolroom and Israel our primary schoolteacher, if we are to come to know the truth of God and humankind, Creator and creature, as it comes in Jesus. For whether we like it or not, the particular place and time of Israel in Palestine is what God chose as the preparative for the Word made (Jewish) flesh, who is the Saviour of all.

Jesus was born out of the womb both of Mary and of Israel. We cannot tear him from that matrix and place him in another culture, at another time and place. He certainly speaks out to all cultures and peoples of all time and every place with the speech of God; but he does so with an Aramaic/Hebrew accent. We recall that the Church of God is built on the foundation not only of the apostles but also of the Hebrew prophets, and also that in the Nicene Creed the Holy Spirit is specifically declared as speaking through these same prophets. We must accept that Jesus is mediated to us in the conceptual and linguistic patterns of the Bible, the Old Testament pointing to and preparing for the New, and the New looking back to and fulfilling the Old. Therefore the particularity of Jesus – the Son of God born the son of Mary at a given time and place out of a specific background – is the crucible into which all our presuppositions and estimates and theories have to be thrown in order to be recast.

We have to allow Jesus to disclose himself to us: we should not dress him in our presuppositions so that he becomes what we want him to be, and says to us what we want to hear from him. Only by allowing him to be to us exactly what he truly is – that is, to employ an objective way of thinking about him, and not force him into theories of our own perception – can we hear him speak to us out of the context of his eternal relations with the Father and the Holy Spirit, which he does out of the context of his earthly time and place. This means that we must be prepared to read and listen to the words of Scripture with humility and faith, so that in and through them we might be encountered by, and encounter for ourselves, the living Word, even Christ himself.

All too often parts of society and the Church have sought to press Jesus into a mould or force him into a structure which is alien to his own nature and being. Today, for example, we hear much in our western society about equality, justice and rights. Many feel that the Church ought to be in the vanguard of the struggle to bring equality, justice and human rights to people the world over. To assist in this purpose, Jesus is presented as the one who stood for these values. True discipleship is then presented as including the struggle to implement them.

Instead of bringing our concepts of equality, justice and rights to the crucible of the particularity of Jesus, we bring Jesus and place him within the crucible of equality, justice and rights as these are generally defined in the latter part of this century. By doing so we encounter not the Christ of the gospels but a Christ of our own making.

Jesus, as the Christ, came to penetrate the darkness of human existence, for there it lies in complete need of remoulding into a right relationship with its Creator. He came to re-create humanity as God's humanity, the humanity God intends us to be, and which we must be if we are to be truly human. However, because people in Palestine were entrenched in their own illusions as to what the Messiah ought to be like and do, he was rejected, tortured and crucified. 'He came unto his own but his own received him not' (John 1:11).

We continue to make the same kind of mistake. We detach Jesus (by adopting a surface perception of what we think he is) from what he really is in himself. Having removed him from his essential and authentic truth as Son of God/son of Mary (the incarnate Word as a Jewish male), we give him a name and a character derived from an ideal, a theory or even a fad, of a given time and culture. He becomes the divine justification for ideas we have gained from other sources. The truly Christian way involves a radical reconstruction of our knowledge: that is, a new way of thinking out of a centre in Christ and not out of what we have already decided about the nature of God and humanity.

Further, it also means a radical reappraisal of the terminology and language we use of Christ and of what he reveals to us: our words must be appropriate to the nature of the truth he is and which he reveals to us. For example, to claim (as people used to do) that 'Jesus Christ was a young and revolutionary social worker' is to speak of him out of context and in a way that is wholly inappropriate. The expressions and words we use must be formed and chosen under the creative and rational compulsion of the truth which is revealed in and by him.

To close this section we need to make reference to recent and continuing discussion concerning the appropriateness of the maleness of Jesus. Some recent writers have put forward two novel positions with respect to the incarnation of the eternal Son. First they have argued that the Word/Logos could just as well have become human being as female, and, as such, have done all that the will of the Father required to redeem the human race. In the second place in considering the actual, historical incarnation they have insisted that maleness is not an essential aspect of the humanity of the Son of God. It is placed alongside such aspects as colour of eyes, weight and height as a secondary feature. Apparently only being human and being Jewish (to connect with the Old Testament) are regarded as primary aspects of the incarnation of the Son.

This type of theologising seems to us to be entirely misdirected. We see the role of theology to be that of being attentive and obedient to both what God has revealed and how he has revealed it. To speculate as to whether the Word could have become female human being is therefore not appropriate. And further, the fact that the Word became human as male is for us an essential aspect of the incarnation; to say otherwise is to negate God's revelation of himself. In the wisdom of God it was deemed fitting and right that the Son become male human being not female. In obedience this point is where we begin. However we may add that it does seem to be, from the human angle, more appropriate and fitting that the Second Person of the Trinity should be revealed in male rather than female form. For if the latter had been the case there would have been what may be described as an anomaly. The revelation of God in human form would have involved two females – the incarnate Logos and her mother. There would have been no role at all for a male since the function of a foster father cannot be judged to be essential.

We wish to affirm that the eternal Son became human being as Jewish male because this was God's will and that, in the light of this divine fact, our vocation is to know God through the serving of this Jesus Christ.

Jesus and appropriate language

The language which we have is appropriate to our status and limitations as created beings. It is bound to the dimension of this world of time and things. We have no language of eternity. This however is not a problem for theology. God has accommodated himself to our limitations in Christ; and in Christ, and under the direction of his unfolding disclosure of himself to be the eternal Son of God born a son of man, our language is appropriately formed from within our limitations.

This propriety of language means that we use terms in a particular way under the compulsion of the objective truth which Christ is. We use terms which, disciplined by the nature of that truth, point beyond their limitations to the inexpressible majesty of the eternal God. Propriety of terminology also means that we must be constantly aware of the fact that we can never comprehend God within that language. Human terms may be helpful to us; they are not fitting to God.

We hold that the images/symbols we use in speaking about God are referred to him and directed to him so that he transcends them to give us by grace a knowledge of himself. They are mere pointers which do not convey their earthly and human content into the eternal existence of God.

There must be a reverent use of images/symbols, and that reverence must be called forth by no other consideration than that of the nature of the God who has revealed himself to us. If any other factor determines the choice and use of images, then we are using God for ulterior ends, and our motives are other than obedience to God. God is utterly beyond all human imagination. For this reason he has divinely selected and divinely arranged images through which he enables us to know him. These divine images are given by God and not chosen by man.

This point came to a head during the fourth-century controversy with the Arians (see ch. 4) and their use and choice of images. The issue centred round the Father/Son relationship of the internal and eternal being of God. The orthodox held that God reveals himself as Father and named himself as such in and through his incarnate Son. We cannot therefore ignore and sidestep the self-naming of God. The words 'Father' and 'Son' are express terms sanctioned by God himself, to which the New Testament so eloquently witnesses.

To suggest that they are inadequate implies two things. First that God's revelation is inadequate, and second that there is a basic ignorance of fundamental doctrine. For not only are these terms commanded by God, but they are so commanded in order that they should have a specific use in our thinking about God. The problem which faced the orthodox in the Arian dispute was how to prevent the earthly and human content residing in the terms 'father' and 'son' from being projected into God, and how to ensure the divine content (given in revelation) was accepted.

They saw the problem clearly in biblical precedent. In the Old Testament, with its prohibition of images to Israel, what was forbidden was the way in which images were used in the surrounding pagan religions. All the content of the images employed in the worship of Baal and the Astaroth were projected into the supposed existence of these deities. These deities were the creatures of that projection of human sexuality in all its forms, and of the fertility rites of nature. That was what the Nicene fathers saw had to be avoided, and equally saw that Arius had opened the door for this sort of projection.

The issue was one of diametrically opposed methods of thinking. In Greek thought, the idea was that a beam of light from the eye gave rational form to the object studied, and knowledge of that object was on that basis. In other words, the eye and the mind were the sources of knowledge. In orthodox thought, what the object really was in itself informed the mind as that object disclosed itself in all its realities. It was the source of knowledge about itself.

Equally the Arian way of thinking was to project human images into the divine. The orthodox saw that the divine had projected his own image into the human at the incarnation. The incarnation was the presentation of THE image of God among humanity. Jesus was THE image of God, for he was what he imaged. Here then, in the relation of the incarnate Son with the eternal Father, was the source and the fullness of knowledge and wisdom in thinking about God.

Jesus is not the personification of what humanity thinks about God, he is God in Person, God the Son who is towards us what he eternally is in himself. He is, as the Nicene fathers pointed out, THE image or form of the Godhead, and this was further strengthened by their doctrine of the Holy Spirit. The Spirit is the image of the Son, but he is invisible. He is both the gift of God and the Giver, for he too is God – the Spirit of the Father and the Son, taking the things of the Son and freely giving them to us. The Father/Son relationship in the Godhead is in the Spirit, and this rules out all bald and immediate application of human images into the Godhead.

The Son and the Spirit, together for us the source of knowledge and enlightenment, are the determiners of the use of images. The determining truth which is the Son's and the Spirit's dictates and moulds the choice and use of images as pointers to them as the truth incarnate and the truth enlightening. There can be no intrusion of images in our minds in thinking about God, alien to the nature of the truth of God revealed in Christ through the Spirit, or inappropriate to the nature of the Son and the Spirit, who, as God, convey that truth.

St Basil (Epistle 125:3) states with regard to baptism into the name of Father, Son and Holy Spirit, 'We are bound to be baptised in the terms we have received and to express belief in the terms in which we have been baptised.'

It is in a spiritual way that we are to employ those images already established by God himself and which have divine sanction. For the existence of, and relation between, Father, Son and Holy Spirit, that is, the doctrine of the Trinity, is without comparison and can only be worshipped and adored and not explained – or even bettered.

Additional note: Is Christ as human being androgynous?

To the ordinary reader of the gospels it seems clear that Jesus was certainly a human being and truly a male both before and after his resurrection from the dead. However there have been voices raised at different times in the history of the Church to claim that in some way Jesus was or now is an androgyne (somehow a being of both sexes).

Following Plato, Origen taught that in the general resurrection of the dead people will be raised as male–female beings. This was judged to be erroneous, and the Church later affirmed that there will be a differentiation of male and female in the final resurrection to everlasting life, though of course in a different state and relation to each other than in the present life. There will be a fulfilment of the complementarity of male and female, but not a cancelling or a confusion of it. In modern times the view that Adam before the fall and Christ after his bodily resurrection were androgynous beings, perfectly combining in themselves the fullness of male and female characteristics and features, is associated with the German mystic, Jakob Boehme (1575–1624). His influence has been immense, and in this idea of the androgynous Adam and Christ, he has been followed by many people including Paul Evdokimov (who also was influenced in this teaching by C. G. Jung): and (via Schelling) the further idea that God is an androgynous deity is reflected in the teaching of Paul Tillich (who attempts to androgynise all three Persons of the Godhead).

Though the intention may appear to be worthy – for example, to present a new Adam and a Christ, not to mention a God, who combined the best of female and male and therefore is entirely suited to be the saviour of both males and females – the doctrine is false. Sexual differentiation is a fundamental aspect of human nature, and though resurrection recreates man's biological nature, it does not abolish it. Further, the maleness of Jesus Christ is an essential part of his human nature, for he thought, willed and acted as a perfect male and as a male Messiah.

His inexchangeable and irreducible maleness does not, however, mean that he can only be and is only the saviour of males. His humanity, expressed as maleness, is recapitulative. That is, because the reality of his humanity was taken into union with the eternal Word by whom all things were created, and given existence in that union, his humanity is effective for all created humanity. He, as the one by whom all things were created, became one of his own creatures, and gathered to himself all time and things, and therefore all humanity. It is the relation of the reality of his humanity to his divinity which is the point of this summing up, this recapitulation – not the breadth of some principle of general humanity which he assumed at his incarnation.

We have to consider also that while sexual differences are basic they are within (not outside of) human nature which exists in male and female forms. In the Father's wisdom and will the Son became male man (human being) in order to become the saviour of the whole human race. He was born a baby boy, grew up to be a Jewish male adult, died on the cross as a man of sorrows, and rose from the dead as immortal male Lord of Glory.

In contrast we can say that Mary his mother, called *theotokos* (God-bearer) by the early Church, was born a baby girl, grew up to be a female Jewish homemaker, died a female Christian, and is regarded by the doctrine of the assumption to have been taken up into heaven as a glorified female body. Her sex was, of course, of absolute importance in her miraculous conception of Jesus as the Word made flesh, for she had to have a womb to bear him. In heaven she is immortalised, but still 'she'.

4

Distorting Revelation

In this chapter we shall consider two examples of the relativising of revelation. Both presentations of God/Christ were extremely attractive to many people on their first appearance, and they enjoyed a temporary triumph before they were eventually rejected as being distortions of the truth of revelation. We provide them by way of cautionary tales. They warn us that when a dominant or vociferous cultural movement invades Christian doctrine it seriously distorts it. Yet they also show us that, despite popular acceptance, sooner or later they are rejected by the majority when their full implications are realised, and they are seen in their true light as erroneous interpretations of revelation.

Arianism

The great problem which the Church of the fourth century AD faced was to teach and proclaim the Hebraic–Christian way of thinking about God and creation, within the culture and outlook of the Graeco–Roman world. The tackling of that problem, which intensified through the teachings of the heretic Arius, resulted in the Council of Nicaea and the Nicene Creed in AD 325, and in the Council of Constantinople which revised the Creed and strengthened it in AD 381.

The root of the problem was the presupposition in Graeco–Roman thought that we can only know what we can see and understand. Only what we can grasp is rational and all else is to be dismissed as irrational. It followed that knowledge of

God can only be knowledge of a God who is within the grasp
of the human mind, and therefore limited and finite. This way
of thinking meant, on the one hand, that God was demeaned
by bringing him into, and keeping him in, the same dimension
as creation, or, on the other hand, creation was elevated into
the same dimension as God, and the limited was therefore
really unlimited and the finite infinite. Behind this lay the
assumption that the human mind is the real final authority and
judge of all.

In this situation the Christian doctrine that all things were
created by the eternal Word or Son of God was particularly
vulnerable to error, unless clearly stated. For at this point there
was concentrated the real issue, distinction and conflict between
the biblical mind of the orthodox fathers of the Church and the
Graeco–Roman attitude. So this doctrine was of fundamental
importance for the establishing of the relation between God
and creation.

The heretic Arius, a priest in Alexandria 312–316, tried to
solve the problem of an infinite God and a finite creation by
bringing down into the created dimension the One by whom
things are made. That is, he regarded the Son of God as the
first and greatest of all created beings, and as such it was by
him that the Father created all things. So there was 'a time
when he was not'. What Arius did was to confuse the way in
which the eternal Son of God existed ('eternally begotten' as
the Creed has it) with the act of creation. This, of course,
was an attempt to compromise Christianity with pagan Greek
thought and culture in which the divine Logos/Word was
regarded as being only and merely the rational principle of
creation, totally confined within it.

What Athanasius and the Nicene fathers of the Church did
was to show that in the eternal relation of the Son to the Father
there is an identity of natures. The Son is of the same God-
ness as the Father ('of one substance', as the Creed has it).
The Father is never without the Son – even as a light always
shines and a river always flows with water. In creation there is
a disparity of natures. Creation is brought into being out of

nothing by the free grace of God. It is given by God an existence and an identity, separate from him yet dependent upon
him for that nature and identity.

The relation between the Father and the Son is an internal
relation within the being of God. It is a relation within the
same quality of God-ness. The relation of creation to God is
an external relation, and the two are qualitatively different.

Athanasius, Bishop of Alexandria 328–373, made a clear
distinction between the Creator and creation, between the eternal being of God and the temporal being of things made. God
is to be respected in his God-ness; creation is to be respected
in its creaturely existence. There is no likeness between them,
and 'God is without comparison'. This sounds as though Athanasius was advocating a total split between God and creation.
But this was far from the case. This is God's creation, and he,
since bringing it into being out of nothing through his Word,
continuously upholds it and sustains it in the rationality of its
creaturely dimension by that same Word. The world is his
handiwork and the sphere of his activity towards us. But in all
this he still remains God, and creation remains in its creaturely
identity and nature.

It is into this sphere of time and things that the Word comes
at the incarnation. The Word comes as man (not in man). He
comes as man without any change or diminution of his divinity.
This means that we can know God as he exists as God, and
we can know him without losing our human identity and being.
We can now think about God out of a centre in God himself
because God has accommodated himself to the limitations of
our creaturely existence in becoming man. And he becomes
man, not by swallowing our humanity or changing it to be other
than a creaturely existence, but by becoming bone of our bone
and flesh of our flesh and mind of our mind. Here is truly
gospel.

We know God in Christ, because of his identification with
our humanity and its limitations. We know God in Christ
because this Jesus is both God – not something less than God,
or something of God, or something about God – and God in all

his God-ness, made man. Athanasius saw that the incarnation meant that something new had taken place in God. Before the incarnation God was only God in God. Now he is also man. This spoke volumes of the sort of God God is. He is not a prisoner of his own eternity. He is not constricted by his deity as some Unmoved Mover, as Aristotle would have him to be. God is so marvellously free in his existence as God that, without ceasing to be what he is eternally, he can 'go outside himself' in the incarnation, and freely act in and towards his creation.

Arius and the Arians thought that the Son or Word was created as the first principle of all things. They brought him down firmly into the realm of created things, which by their nature are changeable. There was no thought of God revealing himself in his Son in such a way that he remains the eternal God yet has respect to the nature of his creation. Because of this, Christ became detached from God and was seen as only a changeable image of God. He was made, therefore, merely the plaything of man's understanding, and could be moulded into whatever fashionable view prevailed. In the Arian approach man's understanding of what is truth and goodness, and all his values, are then imposed on Christ who merely becomes the justification for such human understanding.

In contrast salvation was seen by Athanasius as bringing humanity into a right relationship with God, and re-creating humanity to be what God intends it to be. But that can only be learnt from Christ as he is revealed to us in accordance with what he is as both God and man. Moreover salvation concerns the whole of the individual – not just a soul, but body and mind as well. It is the totality of each person with which God is concerned, and with the renewal of what each person is in the rational order of God's creation.

An important part of this salvation was the renewing of the human mind in Christ, so that it may understand God (and therefore itself in that light) out of a centre in God, and not out of an introverted centre in itself merely justifying itself by irrationally mistreating God. For it is under the loving compulsion of the truth of God as it is in Jesus that our thoughts are led to think rationally about God, and our language about God appropriately formed. Moreover Christ not only ministers, as God, the things of God to humankind but, as man, the things of humankind to God. We find ourselves truly to be what we are in him. We are established in him and therefore we must, we may, live a life in a right and liberating relationship to the God who is towards us in Christ what he eternally is in himself. For he has freely taken our human existence into his own so that we may be truly human – as God's humanity.

Face to face with Jesus Christ we know him, by the disclosure by himself, to be what and who he is. He initiates the conversation with us, determines our mode of thought and creates in our minds human terms which are appropriate to what and who he is, and which point beyond themselves to that indescribable truth, indicating more then they can specify and quantify. A reality creates appropriate vocabulary. The manipulation of vocabulary does not create reality. If it did, this would be mythology.

The method employed by Arius, lifted uncritically out of the cultural norms of the time and forced on Christ, was totally inappropriate to what God is in himself and what he has so revealed in Christ. It had no rational approach corresponding to the reality facing it, and bore all the hallmarks of speculative mythology.

Genuine theology speaks out to culture in its midst, not from culture and dictated by it. The temptation for theology to take the latter course, so that it can be seen to be immediately relevant in the easiest and most palatable way, has been a perennial problem of the Church. In fact one of the battles which the Church has to fight on behalf of the real dignity and honour of humanity (that is, as God's humanity in Christ and the lasting values of humanity which repose in that Christ) is against a bogus mystique of culture. This requires to be demythologised and unmasked of its false divinity before it can really be called human culture.

Nowhere is this battle fiercer and more dangerous than when God has been dragged in, Arian fashion, with the images and forms which society throws up about itself projected on to him, to justify what society already thinks about itself and to bless the way in which society has already decided it will move.

This was clearly seen by Christian theologians in the Germany of the 1930s.

National socialism

The culture generated by the Nazi philosophy sought to be all-embracing in the Germany of the 1930s. It attempted to bring Jesus Christ within its presuppositions and parameters, and it seemed attractive and 'right' to millions of Germans of the time.

The general plan was to make Jesus Christ serve German nationalism and Nazi culture by transforming him into a German Messiah. So while his historical existence was affirmed, his Jewishness and commitment to the Jewish people as their Messiah was ignored, denied or distorted. It was a case where Jesus was brought in to assist Nazi propaganda, and where the latter became the arbiter of what could be read out of the gospels and out of the Christian tradition, and therefore of what and who Christ was. Appeal was made to the first article of the Apostle's Creed as well as to the 'ordinances of creation' in order to produce a virtually pagan form of natural and civic religion – *Blut und Boden! Ein Volk, ein Reich, ein Führer* – in which the rulers usurped the place of God (whose instruments and servants they were supposed to be). Hitler himself was baptised and confirmed. Thus for much of the German Church in this period Christ was 'the Christ of culture'. This cultural Christ was a tall, blond, Teutonic male with blue eyes, offering a this-worldly salvation to Caucasian peoples.

God always has his faithful ones who will not follow the prevailing fashion and deny their Lord. Led by Karl Barth, a group of German pastors and theologians protested at the intrusion of what they called natural theology into the teaching of the Church. The natural theology which they attacked was that which supposedly stands as an independent way to, and means of, the knowledge of God, apart from Christ, and indeed behind the back of Christ. There is of course a very proper natural theology, in which creation is looked at in the light of what Christ has done – so that the darkness of creation and its 'groaning and travailing' are seen to point, as a parable, to Christ's passion, and the beauty and harmony of creation as a parable to what creation has already become, though as yet hidden from open sight, in his resurrection and ascension – the new heaven and the new earth.

But Barth and his colleagues were concerned with a natural theology which claims that God and the things of God can be read instantly and automatically from the present forms of the world and from the authority of human cultural achievement. Christology, they saw, had become merely the pliable servant to this natural theology. They refused to turn a blind eye to the perversion of Christology in the service of German nationalism and cultural aspirations. The Confessional Synod of the German Evangelical Church met in Barmen, 29 to 31 May 1934, in order to withstand in faith and unity the attack upon the orthodox confession of faith, and to insist that all true doctrine of Christ is based on God's revelation set forth in Holy Scripture. They produced what has become known as the Theological Declaration of Barmen, 1934. Here are the first and second theological statements of that short Declaration:

1 [John 14:6; 10:1, 9 are quoted.] Jesus Christ, as he is attested for us in Holy Scripture, is the one Word of God which we have to hear and which we have to trust and obey in life and in death.

   We reject the false doctrine, as though the Church could and would have to acknowledge as a source of its proclamation, apart from and besides this one Word of God, still other events and powers, figures and truth, as God's revelation.

2 [1 Cor. 1:30 is quoted.] As Jesus Christ is God's assurance of the forgiveness of all our sins, so in the same way and

with the same seriousness he is also God's mighty claim upon our whole life. Through him befalls us a joyful deliverance from the godless fetters of this world for a free, grateful service in his creatures.

We reject the false doctrine, as though there were areas of our life in which we would not belong to Jesus Christ but to other lords – areas in which we would not need justification and sanctification through him.

The third statement emphasises that the Church belongs to the Lord Jesus, and is to proclaim his Word – not any prevailing ideology. The fourth insists that church officers are to serve the congregations under the lordship of Christ. The fifth sets out the vocation of the State under God, and rejects claims to totalitarianism. Finally the sixth statement proclaims the vocation of the Church to serve Christ in word and sacrament.

In his *Church Dogmatics* (vol. II:1) Barth declares that the teaching of the German Christians was a Trojan horse, as the claims of natural theology to have a place in humanity's knowledge of God always are and have been. He stresses that the Declaration of Barmen set out to tackle the problem of natural theology, which threatened to become the norm for Church life, theology and proclamation. It had ever been the claim of natural theology that side by side with the revelation of God in Christ, the Church should also recognise and give place to revelation in reason, in the emotions, and in culture with its achievements and developments.

This 'also' all too soon became apparent as 'only': 'A natural theology which does not strive to be the only master is not a natural theology' (ibid. p. 173). Full sovereignty is the aim of the makers of this Trojan horse. It manifests itself apparently innocuously and attractively by the introduction of a hyphen or the word 'and' – 'modern-positive', 'religious-social', 'community-worship'. The very acknowledgement of such combinations is the beginning of an inclined plane on which the 'also' gathers momentum into full force and impact. These are the points which Barth sets out, and from the particular historical setting which he recalls and round which he places them we go on to look at this 'also' and what it generally implies in any culture and time.

The argument for this 'also' is that it is timely, it makes the gospel relevant, it establishes points of contact with the secular world. It is also possessed with the subtle pretence that it makes the gospel wider than the orthodox proclamation of theology permits. It speaks of a God who has regard for the glory of humanity, the development of culture, and social and moral concepts which are universally applicable.

But we must ask where these high-minded concepts have their origin. By what authority do they operate? We must answer that they are invariably the product of a dualistic way of thinking where Creator and creature, eternity and time, heavenly and earthly, spiritual and material, have been wren- ched apart. They stem from an observational interpretation of humanity and humanity's circumstances. They represent views which take no account of God's revelation. They are therefore an understanding of humanity out of itself, and contain no reference to its true nature as created and redeemed by God.

God is construed as that which corresponds to this human- centred understanding and its attendant values, and, because our Lord is also interpreted by mere observation and idealised theory, he is made, in Arian fashion, the highest instance of that created dimension. He is torn away from the matrix of his true nature as Son of God/son of Mary, the eternal Son of God born in the fullness of time out of the womb of Israel, and made to serve passing causes. But these passing causes and the self-regarding introversion which has given rise to them cannot deal with the profound issues of the relation between Creator and creature, eternity and time, life and death. They can only see and function within the boundaries of human limitations, and God is indeed, via Christ, dragged in to justify findings made on that basis – a basis which has become divinised and which it is heresy to question.

All who rest on this basis have, like the Arians, relativised revelation, and their authority is not the Christ who reveals himself, but rather their own understanding.

Summary

The history of the Church of God provides many examples of the relativising of revelation. They all spring from the same well of natural theology with its defective ways of thinking of observational and idealised theories. We have looked at only two from different centuries and places. However they are sufficient to make our point.

Later we shall seek to show that what is occurring in the adoption of feminine/inclusive language for God (as it does in the opposite, erroneous view that present language implies a male God) is yet another – and very serious – example of that relativising of revelation. In fact it often amounts to the denial or rejection of revelation through the claim that the central teaching/core of the New Testament is totally culturally conditioned.

5

Revelation and the Father

We begin with a summary of some of the important points we have tried to make in previous chapters.

The terms we use to describe and address God must be formed under the creative and rational compulsion of the truth which reveals itself to be what it actually is. We are not free to invent our own! In fact this is true in any field of study. We would not use biological language to describe the workings of an internal combustion engine, or engineering language to describe a plant or animal.

When people take a merely observational and surface way of looking at Jesus, they detach him from the ultimate being of God and bring his divine nature within the confines of the created dimension and therefore under the descriptive ability of the human mind. Also, when Jesus has been detached from his essential historical context he can then be manipulated by various cultural-bound propagandists, and dressed in the biases of what they already think about God.

The terms and language which we use about Jesus and God have to be controlled from the objective reality which is of himself. We must now look at what this implies for particular terms or verbal images/symbols which we use about God.

The use of images/symbols

One of the most important developments in the Old Testament prohibited the making of images. This was because the pagan mind expressed in the image what was thought about the god concerned. The image embodied the truth about that god, and there was a direct link between the image and the god itself. In other words the image had become the god. But the image was merely a projection and an embodiment of human values or aspirations, and we have here a confusion between truth and verbal images or statements about truth.

Statements or verbal images about truth only point to the truth, and are of themselves totally inadequate fully to describe and contain the truth. They point away from themselves to what is greater than they can ever be. This has always been recognised by the Church. 'God is without comparison,' said St Athanasius in the midst of the battle which the Church of the fourth century had to fight with the Arian heresy on precisely this point.

We cannot project a verbal image which pictures what we think of humanity's nature and being into God. That is merely to bring God in to justify what we already think. The Arians did this. By removing Christ's one-ness with the Father and the Spirit and bringing his divinity down into the dimension of a created thing, they thought that they could push their views of human sexuality via Jesus into the eternal being of God. They manipulated Jesus to get at God, and ended up with a bisexual God.

In contrast what we should do (if we work in a rational way with the revelation of God who is towards us in Jesus what he eternally is in himself) is to lay all our terms and language under the refining power of the truth as it is in Jesus, and let them be recast and remoulded there. Then all our verbal images will properly serve this Jesus Christ who is the true image of God, for he is what he 'images'. He is the only permissible image which is complete in itself, for he is what he reflects. Our verbal images are to be the obedient servants of that truth which he is, not the determining masters of it.

The verbal images of our language have to be used in such a way that they point away from themselves, acknowledging their own inadequacy, to the God who cannot be imaged; for he is beyond all created being and is without comparison in this dimension of time and things. It is only as God enters this world of time and place in the integrity and wholeness of the truth of what he is in himself, that we can have the means of working out (in as far as the limitations of language allow) the proper and correct way to employ verbal images. The way is opened out by him as in humility we acknowledge our inadequacy before him. Our relation to God is an imageless relation, where our language is to be used in such a way that it does not compromise God within the confines of its limitations. Before examining the term 'Father', we can note this relation by considering the term 'person'.

The use of the term 'person'

We tend to look at the word 'person' as though it meant an isolated individual, complete and full in himself/herself. This is because of our modern, western habit of looking at the surface of things and making up hard-and-fast, mechanical theories about them, and then applying these theories in practice.

But orthodox Christianity learnt early on, from the way in which it understood the truth in Jesus, that 'person' meant something rather and more radically different. A 'person' was not an entity which could be regarded as existing in isolation and self-sufficiency. The 'person' of the eternal Son of God, while having his own identity, existed in inseparable union with the 'persons' of the Father and the Holy Spirit.

This Son of God is the 'personalising person', for all human persons (and all things) are created by him, depend on him and have their fulfilment in him. He is their source, their sustainer and their destiny. Human persons exist, therefore, in dependence on the Son or Word of God, both for their creation and re-creation and true identity: 'Our life is hid with Christ in God.' It is only by reference to him that we can be the persons we really are, and exist as we can only truly exist.

Moreover just as he as proper Person exists in company with the Father and the Holy Spirit, so humanity, created in the image (not as the image) of God, points beyond itself to that God, in the diversity yet unity of its personhood. That is, humanity, created as male person and female person bound in mutual love and respect – 'not confusing the persons or dividing the substance' – images in a temporal fashion the existence of the eternal God as Father and Son in the bond of eternal love which is the Holy Spirit.

Now obviously, if we apply a mechanistic view of 'person' by projecting that, unrefined, crudely into the eternal being of God, we project our human sexuality, with all that that implies, our human divisions and our human limitations. The essential being of the Trinity is then destroyed, and absurdities arise such as the fact that in this way of thinking and working, God logically must have a grandfather, and so on *ad absurdum*.

We must stop forcing God into our cultural generalities, and listen to what we may learn from the particularity of the truth which determines and properly shapes the existence of all things as that truth which is in Christ. It is in Christ that we learn of the concept 'person' as it is established in the relation he has with the Father. In Christ we have immediately the unfolding of the doctrine of the Trinity and, in the light of these Persons and their eternal relation, the entrance into an understanding of what 'person' as applied to humanity means.

We wish to show that Father is the name by which God both chose and chooses to be known. It is God's self-naming, and this we cannot ignore. The first Person of the Trinity is to be known by this name, and this speaks clearly of the sort of Person he is. We intend to provide the biblical foundation for the addressing of this God by the Church over nearly twenty centuries as 'Our Father who art in heaven'. We shall begin by noting how Jesus addressed God.

Jesus and the Father

The word Father occurs 170 times on the lips of Jesus in the gospels. In terms of the size and vocabulary of the gospels, this is a staggering statistic. It emphasises eloquently just how basic in early Christianity was this term for addressing God in worship and prayer. Further (and this is remarkable in the context of Judaism) Jesus invoked God as Father in his own recorded prayers, with the exception of the cry of dereliction from the cross (which is quotation from Ps. 22:1; see Mark 15:34; Matt. 27:46). We shall notice these prayers as they are recorded in the gospels of St Luke and St John.

1   (Luke 10:21) After the return of the seventy-two disciples from their mission to the Jews, Jesus rejoiced in the Holy Spirit and prayed: 'I thank thee, Father, Lord of Heaven and earth, that thou hast hidden these things from the wise and understanding and revealed them to babes; yea, Father, for such was thy gracious will.'

2   (Luke 22:42) In the Garden of Gethsemane just before his trial and crucifixion, Jesus prayed: 'Father, if thou art willing, remove this cup from me; nevertheless not my will, but thine, be done.'

3   (Luke 23:34) On the cross Jesus prayed for those who crucified him: 'Father, forgive them; for they know not what they do.'

4   (Luke 23:46) As he expired on the cross, Jesus prayed: 'Father, into thy hands I commend my spirit!'

5   (John 11:41–2) At the tomb of Lazarus, Jesus prayed: 'Father, I thank thee that thou hast heard me. I knew that thou hearest me always'.

6   (John 12:28) Not long before his trial and crucifixion Jesus prayed: 'Father, glorify thy name.'

7   (John 17:1) Just before his trial and crucifixion, Jesus prayed for his disciples, beginning in this way: 'Father the hour has come; glorify thy Son that the Son may glorify thee'.

The term Father also occurs in John 17:5, 11, 21, 24, 25, as an address by Jesus to God.

Alongside the prayers we must place that teaching of Jesus in which he speaks so naturally of God's relationship to him as that of Father to Son. The gospel of John is of course rich in this material (for example 8:12ff; 10:22ff; 14:1–16:33). But it is not absent from the Synoptic Gospels. Take as an instance this claim of Jesus: 'All things have been delivered to me by my Father; and no one knows the Son except the Father, and no one knows the Father except the Son and any one to whom the Son chooses to reveal himself' (Matt. 11:27; Luke 10:22). Semitic in form, this saying has a context of meaning within the Jewish home where there was an intimate relationship between father and son. The father initiated his son both into the content of the Torah and into the secrets of his craft or trade. Jesus tells us that everything has been handed on by his Father in heaven, and that because of this he alone truly knows the Father and is able to make the Father known to others.

Scholars agree that the actual word which Jesus used was the Aramaic *Abba*. This had its origin as a word young children used of their fathers – something like 'Daddy' in English. It came also to be used within the large family circle by children (whatever their age) of their father and, by all, of older men as an expression of courtesy. It was a word from everyday speech and as far as we know Jesus was the first Jew to address the Lord God in heaven by this term of endearment. It has been rightly claimed that the use of *Abba* reveals the heart of Jesus' relationship to God and to the meaning and essence of the kingdom of God. In fact it is so fundamental to the identity and mission of Jesus – who he was as the eternal Son of God and what he did as this, born the son of Mary – that it is inconceivable that it could be replaced or removed. To do so would be to remove the very essential of the revelation and reconciliation of God in and by Jesus.

The disciples and the Father

Not only did Jesus address the Lord God as Father, he also taught his disciples to do so. When asked for guidance in how to pray, Jesus took a benediction from the synagogue liturgy and transformed it by the addition of 'Father'. This benediction went as follows: 'Glorified and sanctified be his great name in the world which he created according to his will. May his kingdom come in your lifetime and in your days, and in the lifetime of the whole house of Israel, soon and without delay. And to this say: Amen.'

The prayer Jesus taught went like this: 'Father [*Abba*], hallowed be thy name. Thy kingdom come. Give us each day our daily bread; and forgive us our sins, for we ourselves forgive every one who is indebted to us; and lead us not into temptation.'

In its longer, Matthean form, this prayer has been prayed by every generation of Christians since the foundation of the Church by the apostles. The privilege and joy of disciples addressing God as 'our Father' was at the core of Jesus' teaching. This is seen not only in his provision of the Lord's Prayer, but also in the important catechetical teaching he gave his followers. It is to be noted that the phrase 'our Father' means that we pray in company with Jesus. The Father, strictly, is his Father alone, for he is the eternally begotten Son of that Father. But in his solidarity with us, as our brother in the incarnation, bone of our bone and flesh of our flesh and mind of our mind, we are adopted through him, and pray in company with him. We make our prayers through the mouth of Christ where, in our risen humanity, he is beside our Father and pleads in that humanity for us – his Father and through him ours. That is why we end our prayers with 'through Jesus Christ our Lord', for we pray through him and with him and by him and in him.

In his teaching, Jesus gives us an entrance to the Father, so that he says 'your Father'. For example:

1 (Mark 11:25) 'Whenever you stand praying, forgive, if you have anything against any one; so that your Father also who is in heaven may forgive you your trespasses.'
2 (Matt 5:48) 'But you are to be perfect, as your Father in heaven is perfect.'

3   (Luke 12:32) 'Fear not, little flock, for it is your Father's good pleasure to give you the kingdom.'

We may claim that Father is the name for the God to whom the disciples are to pray. He is the sovereign Lord who is holy and compassionate, who forgives our sins, provides all our needs, and brings us to fulfilment and maturity in his kingdom. From this base it is easy to understand why Jesus set aside the usual custom, and bade his disciples to call no one on earth *Abba* (that is, to call no older man *Abba* as a term of respect). Nevertheless such a remarkable prohibition points to the exceeding importance of *Abba* as God's name.

When we turn to the letters of the apostle Paul, we find that he unhesitatingly calls God 'Father', as the introductory words in all his letters make clear: 'From God our Father and the Lord Jesus Christ'. Further, he describes the Christian life as being membership of the family of God. He wrote:

> For in Christ Jesus you are all sons of God, through faith. For as many of you as were baptised into Christ have put on Christ. There is neither Jew nor Greek, there is neither slave nor free, there is neither male nor female; for you are all one in Christ Jesus (Gal. 3:26–28). You have received the spirit of sonship. When we cry 'Abba! Father!' it is the Spirit himself bearing witness with our spirit that we are children of God, and if children, then heirs, heirs of God and fellow heirs with Christ, provided we suffer with him in order that we may also be glorified with him. (Rom. 8:15–17)

St Paul teaches that what Jesus Christ, the Lord, does is to enable believing sinners to share in his filial relationship with the Father through the action of the Holy Spirit. Because of this unique relationship between the Father and the Son in the Spirit, and because of the special work of the Spirit, human beings are united to the Son in faith, and thereby become the adopted sons of God and members of the family of God. Both males and females become the adopted sons of God and, as sons, are the recipients of the privileges and blessings which come to such sons. Together in prayer and worship they address God as 'our Father' and do so 'through Jesus Christ our Lord'.

The Old Testament and Jewish background

First it is apparent that in the Old Testament the use of the word Father for God is basically metaphorical. That is, certain (admirable) characteristics of human fatherhood are applied to God so that the Lord is said to be like a human father in certain respects. God guides, leads and disciplines Israel as a father his son (Deut. 1:31; 8:5; Ps. 103:13; Hose. 11:1–4; Jer. 31:9, 20).

Then also he acts as an adoptive father with reference to the king whom, having chosen, he both blesses and chastens (2 Sam. 7:8–16; Ps. 2:7). Israel/its king, as God's son, is a further metaphor linked to that of God as father. Here the son is seen as being dependent upon, and owing obedience to, the father – that is, faithful to the covenant which bound them to their God, for Israel as 'my son' was called out of Egypt (Hos. 11:1). We must also add that only those who were a part of Israel and who recognised their covenant position before God could truly know in mind and heart what it meant to call God 'Father of Israel'.

However if we were to paint a verbal picture of the position of the father in a typical Jewish home before and during the life of Jesus, and then transfer to God the essential characteristics of that fatherhood, we would not be presenting the God whom Jesus addressed as *Abba*. We would be presenting a male deity, totally committed to his world and human family, but authoritarian, and with a greater concern for the male than the female members of his house. This is the kind of God some recent writers have assumed to be required if we use the term 'Father'. We just do not begin with the concept of fatherhood (in any time or culture) and apply that to God. That is to fit God into a framework of our own understanding, and interpret him according to our norms and experience. This is a flawed

way of thinking indeed. Let us suppose a teacher tells a class
to think of their fathers and try to imagine God like that. What
of the child whose father arrives home drunk each night and
beats the mother? What sort of God is being presented to that
child? Or what of the child with a drunken mother, if 'mother'
is likewise applied to God? We simply cannot project human
images into the nature of the eternal God. That is the tendency
of Arianism.

The word 'Father' on the lips of Jesus is to be understood
primarily in terms of the context of teaching by Jesus himself.
That is, we are to understand it as it comes to us in that
revelation from God which is in, through, by and with Jesus
Christ. Certainly this context includes the witness of the Old
Testament to God as Father and gains meaning from the reality
of human fatherhood in human society – in this case Jewish
society. However we do not begin with the Jewish patriarchy
and read into God features of that human system (whether
they be good or bad by contemporary judgment) in order to
ascertain what the being God the Father is all about. Rather
we begin from the words of Jesus and seek to understand them
in the context which he supplies by word and deed.

Alongside the metaphor of fatherhood in the Old Testament,
we must also add the (much less common) use of motherhood
(in birds and humans) to describe God. However it is at the
level not of true metaphor, but of simile. (Simile, we may
recall, differs from metaphor in that it merely and only states
resemblance, while metaphor declares that one thing is like
another.) On several occasions, God's care for Israel is com-
pared to that of a mother bird for its young. God's compassion
is like that of an eagle that stirs up its nest, flutters over its
young, spreads out its wings and catches them, bearing them on
its pinions (Deut. 32:11; Isa. 32:1–5). Then on four occasions in
the latter part of the Book of Isaiah there are feminine similes
for God – the cry of childbirth (42:14), the actual bringing to
birth (45:10), a mother's compassion for her child (49:15) and
a mother's comfort for her child (66:13). That is, God is said
to be like a woman in that he cries out in anguish for his

covenant people, he chooses them and makes them his covenant nation, he loves them with compassion and when they are in trouble he brings them comfort.

Reflection

God the Father is not a 'male' deity. In fact there is no hint of sexuality in God as God. In his eternal being God is beyond all created being, with its limitations, demarcations and distinctions. He is not however beyond all being, for he is the Creator, sustainer and bringer into fulfilment of all that is. The eternal being of God, and the interior relations within that eternal being (the mode of existence of the Trinity), are beyond mortal comprehension and description. They are 'ineffable'. We can say, on the basis of revelation, that the Father and the Son have a perfect union and fellowship and share the same 'substance', the same god-ness. The idea that the Son is the uniquely begotten Son of the Father says nothing whatsoever about the origin or procreation of the Son (for no mother is even hinted at). Rather it is a device to emphasise the sharing of one and the same divine nature. It is generally accepted that *monogenes* (John 1:14) means 'unique' rather than 'only-begotten'. Thus the Father–Son metaphor points to intimacy rather than generation. This becomes abundantly clear in the prayer of Jesus recorded in John 17, where intimate union is claimed to have existed before the creation of the world. However since the Son is incarnate as Jesus the Messiah, he is the incarnate Son/Word made flesh submitted to the will of the Father in order to fulfil his vocation as the Saviour of the world.

When we reflect upon our addressing God as 'our Father' we soon realise that no sexuality is implied in God. For the Father whom Jesus represents to us is the God who is the holy Father, the compassionate Father, the adopting Father, the Father of all mercies and all providence. There is in this Father divine characteristics which – at the human level – we would call feminine virtues or qualities. For example, compassion and

patience which we believe to be in God but which we attribute
more – in their human form – to women than men.

So while God is presented as having (what we deem to be)
the best female qualities, this God is nevertheless called Father
and never Mother. There was in the world in which the tribes
of Israel lived much religion associated with female and mother
deities. And in some forms of Gnosticism which appeared soon
after Jesus, there were various types of female and hermaphro-
dite deities. Yet both Judaism and Christianity kept themselves
totally free from any suggestion that God, the Lord, could be
called 'our Mother'.

To intrude into the biblical portrayal of the eternal Father,
the incarnate Son and the adopted sons (male and female) the
further picture of God as mother or God as parent is to distort
the whole fine balance of the content of revelation. It is to
introduce sexuality where none was intended, and it is to lose
the revealed doctrine of the Triunity of God, Father, Son and
Holy Spirit.

For we delve into the New Testament and find that, in Jesus'
use of 'my Father', 'our Father', 'your Father', language is
being stretched by its normal use in this created dimension of
time and things, and the word Father used beyond those lexical
and literal definitions. God is not equivalent to any human
father. To speak of *Abba* in the new covenant is to enter the
language of intimate spiritual union, prayer, worship, trust,
commitment and obedience. It is a word spoken from the mind
within the heart under the compelling light of revelation, and it
is a word of the faith, hope and love evoked by that revelation.

We do not need to analyse an exemplary father-figure in
order to discern what are the qualities of God as Father; rather
the God whom we encounter in and through Jesus by the Holy
Spirit is our Father who has so named himself. This self-naming
of God we cannot better or change, otherwise we intrude our
understanding into the prerogative of God. This Father is the
source of all fatherhood: 'I kneel before the Father, from whom
all fatherhood in heaven and earth derives its name,' wrote St
Paul (Eph. 3:14).

In calling God Father we are using language at full stretch, going beyond all normal dictionary meanings so as to establish in a bold manner a fuller representation (but not representation) of deity. The word Father points beyond itself to a fuller and inexpressible content in God which can never been contained within human image/symbols and theories. For God is not equivalent to any human father; he is unique and the source of human fatherhood. This use of Father by Jesus and his disciples may be further classified as making a unique and specific use of foundational symbols and images. There is a particular choice of such, and they are set apart for a particular use. It is so much an integral part of the revelation of which the New Testament is the record and witness that to remove it would be to discard the whole.

We may point out that the essential content, horizon and goal of the words and language of the Bible is both the person of the Word made flesh and all that he opens out for us concerning the knowledge of God. All biblical terminology is a pointer beyond itself to this reality, for its unique status is by God's design to be the witness to the incarnate Word.

The distinguished Scottish theologian T. F. Torrance puts it like this in *The Mediation of Christ* (Paternoster Press, 1983):

> Let me refer to a point of crucial importance where the Jewish mind can help us, in our need to gain a way of thinking of God in which we do not project our creaturely images into God. This is a way of thinking which has been built into Jewish minds at least from Mosaic promulgation of the Second Commandment, forbidding Jews to make any kind of image of God, physical or mental. This is to say, through the self-mediation of divine revelation in Israel a way of knowing God was steadily inculcated in which the creaturely images used in its communications such as are carried by the terms 'father' and 'son' were not projected into God, far less the creaturely sex-content of these images. The Hebrew language is replete with vivid dramatic images, for example, in which feminine feelings are applied to God,

but the relations between these images and God is an image-less relation. The images used are referred to the invisible God imagelessly.

And he continues by referring to scientific inquiry:

The importance of this way of thinking can be shown from its transference to scientific inquiry, in relativity theory or quantum theory, for example, where we are concerned with objective realities that are quite non-observable, and where we have to decipher the information content of invisible light signals that pervade and illuminate the whole universe. We naturally use English, German, French or some other langu-age, all of which are full of images and figures drawn from the observable world, in our inquiries, so that we have to learn how to use languages of this kind without projecting the images they carry into the realm of invisible space–time, electromagnetic waves, or quirks, for that would be a crude mistake. It is significant that at these junctures in modern scientific investigation where we have to penetrate into the invisible intelligible structures in this world, it is very fre-quently Jewish scientists who have led the way. They have helped us break through the screen of the phenomenalist world of appearances with which we have become obsessed in our European tradition in science and philosophy. Thus instead of interpreting the invisible in terms of the visible . . . we have had to do the very opposite: interpret what is visible from what is inherently invisible.

Finally he shows the theological implications of this methodology:

That radical change in scientific thought cannot but have a salutary and cleansing effect upon our biblical scholarship and our theological inquiry, where we have to do finally and above all with God who like light is intrinsically invisible, but in whose light we see light. It can help us to take a hard critical look at ourselves in the conflict between our alien presuppositions and the way God has chosen to make himself known through Israel, to appreciate in a new way the permanent value of the structures of thought with which he has provided us in the mediation of that knowledge, and thus help to bring us back to the biblical way of understanding God in the whole field of his activity in creation and redemption, and of course to a way of interpreting the Holy Scriptures without projecting the creaturely content of our conceptual and linguistic images into God. (pp. 30, 311)

We now turn to a consideration of language applied to humanity.

6

Inclusive Language for Human Beings

We appreciate the reason for the publication in January 1989 of the booklet, *Making Women Visible: the use of inclusive language with the ASB*, from the Liturgical Commission of the Church of England. It helps us to know what we are talking about when we use the expression 'inclusive language' (or 'non-exclusive' language) and what changes are necessary to make the Alternative Service Book (1980) conform to the demands of this inclusive language. We entirely welcome the Commission's decision to leave the Book of Common Prayer (1662) in its received form.

The complexity of the problem

Once the attempt is begun to eliminate what is now called sexist language with reference to human beings from an official liturgy of the Church, those deeply involved soon begin to recognise that the problem is complex, in fact exceedingly complex. For it involves making judgments on matters of psychology and linguistics as well as on culture and theology. Further, the call for inclusive language is itself a very modern theme and the extent to which (and the form in which) it will be heard in a decade or longer is difficult to judge. This is because it is such an obviously culturally conditioned call and it is impossible to predict how it will develop. We recognise this, but it must be affirmed again that our task is that of serving theology and then, and only then, speaking out to other concerns which certainly must be taken into account.

First, we recognise that there are Christian women who feel psychologically hurt by the use of the exclusive language of the liturgy in its traditional form. A typical hurtful sentence from the ASB is 'and to live in love and peace with all men': another is 'we have sinned against you and against our fellow men, in thought, word and deed'. They feel that by such language they are being treated as second-class members of the Church and in the family of God. They – with their supporters – insist that all men and women are equal in dignity before God, and that this ought to be reflected in the words of worship and prayer.

In the second place we recognise that English is a worldwide language, with regional dialects. Of the latter, British and North American English are the biggest, and within each there are regional variations (which also may be called dialects). We are particularly concerned here with British English, though we have an especial interest in North American as well. In British English we need to distinguish between what may be called class-dialects, which vary according to the social class of the person. The Registrar General for England and Wales, in making his decennial census returns, has divided the population into five broad social classes and indicated what percentage of the total falls into each group. We refer to this to make two points.

First, broadly, each of these categories uses a different register of vocabulary, grammar and syntax. Secondly the call for the removal of sexist language from the liturgy comes from women and men in the first two of the Registrar's categories (those with high professions and those with general professional qualifications), comprising about 31 per cent of the total population. As far as we can tell there is little interest in this topic in the other three categories (skilled, semi-skilled and manual workers), and very few, if any, from these categories in attending Church services feel hurt or offended by sexist language.

We notice that despite much pressure and publicity from the media for the removal of sexist language, the term 'man' (used in the singular and without the definite or indefinite article) persists to denote the human race, the species or any member of it, without distinction or gender. There appears to be no satisfactory alternative in most cases to the use of 'man' with this meaning.

Take the Nicene Creed and the traditional translation of *enanthropesanta*/*et homus factus est* as 'and was made man'. It would be correct to render the Greek/Latin as 'and became a human being', but not only is the wording inelegant, it also misses a theological point: this is the anti-Apollinarian content of the Greek verb chosen by the bishops at the Councils of Nicaea and Constantinople. They were insistent that the eternal Son took to himself the totality of human existence, body and mind, without any idea of the human mind being replaced by, or becoming, the mind of the eternal Word (Apollinarius taught that in Jesus the human mind was missing, being replaced by the divine mind). The verb 'made' and the noun 'man' (in the generic sense), in this juxtaposition, indicate the assumption – that is, the 'taking on' – of the fullness of humanity, with full respect to what humanity in essence is, rather than being 'turned into' some sort of epitome of what we have already decided a human being is.

Let us look first at the verbs 'become' and 'made'. The danger that we must be aware of here is the understanding of the English verb 'become'. In ordinary speech it can indicate 'be turned into'. If it is used in this sense for the process of incarnation, then we are indeed in an Arian situation, where the eternal Son/Word of God is transformed into a creature – albeit the first and best of creatures – and is therefore vulnerable to the dictates and relativities of cultural change, for the very possibility of transformation means that he is within this dimension of time and things, and can be manipulated accordingly.

Again another danger is that we try to maintain the God-ness of the eternal Son in the incarnation, but compromise the full humanity of what he took from the Virgin Mary in 'becoming', in order to square it with what we think would be fitting for God to become. The heretic Apollinarius, with the best intention in the world, correctly saw that the human mind was the instrument of humanity's constant rejection of God. Therefore, he argued, God could have nothing to do with a human mind, and in order to save humanity God must replace the human mind with his divine mind. So at the incarnation the eternal Son of God took a human body, and replaced the mind with his Godly mind. On this basis, the humanity taken by the eternal Son at the incarnation was incomplete.

This led to the clause clung to by the fathers of the early Church that 'not assumed means not healed'. They realised that if the eternal Son in the incarnation did not take to himself a human body, flesh, blood and bones, the human body is not healed in re-creation. If he did not take to himself a human mind, the human mind is not re-created and orientated towards God, in which position it rests and finds its rationality.

'Was made' is the most suitable verb to indicate that the One by whom all things were made took to himself the limitations of our mortal dimension – sharing our constrictions, made of the same metal of which we are made and cast in the same mould as us. It preserves the integrity of both the God-ness and the humanity of our Lord and their inseparable but unconfused union in the harmony of that one Jesus Christ. The One by whom all things were created assumed his created reality and was made one of his own creatures.

Now let us look at the noun 'man'. Here we appeal to St Paul in his fifth chapter of the letter to the Romans. The apostle speaks of a summing up of all humanity in Adam, and a greater summing up of all humanity in Jesus Christ, the 'second Adam'. The use of 'man' here is comprehensive, for the name Adam in Hebrew, in any case, means humanity. Adam, in the narrative of Genesis, is the recapitulation of us all, male and female. We are 'Adamic'. But, more importantly and substantially, we are 'in Christ'. What our Lord did in taking the reality of our frailty and mortality in its totality – our Adamic nature – to himself at the incarnation, was to re-create it in all that he was and did, into the new Adam, the new humanity. Our real identity is hid with him in God. The noun 'man' refers to our recapitulation, our solidarity, in Adam in the first instance, but more importantly in Christ in a greater and eternal reality. The eternal has taken our temporality and lovingly made it to be in perfect union with himself. Adam and Christ are the first and last words in inclusive language.

The substitution of any other term – adding the female or trying to eradicate distinction between male and female – only intrudes our divisions and blurs the essential remaking, renewing and recapitulation of us all in that second Adam. It should be noted that the fathers of the early Church were precise in their choice of words concerning the humanity assumed by the eternal Word at the incarnation. The Greek word used was *anthropos* and not *aner* (that is, 'man', but not signifying 'male') and the Latin word *homo* not *vir* (with the same distinction). We must ask that the time-tried and time-tested usage of 'man' be regarded with understanding – not by trying to better it on the one hand by additional female terms, nor on the other by trying to read into it (as so many women in their protest have correctly pointed out) masculinity only. Such attempts only project our divisions and resentments into the being and act of God made man.

The case for theologically permissible change of language is somewhat different, with the earlier phrase in this Creed, *di hemas tous anthropous/propter nos homines* translated as 'for us men'. Nothing would be lost here – except perhaps elegance – if we said 'for our mortal race'. However if we turn to the doctrinally sound and popular hymns of the Church, then we find that in some cases there is just no alternative to the retention of 'man' in its generic sense. Take, for example, lines from Charles Wesley's 'Hark, the herald angels sing':

> Hail the incarnate Deity!
> Pleased as Man with man to dwell,
> Jesus, our Emannuel.

Also the profession of faith of John Henry Newman:

> Firmly I believe and truly
> God is Three and God is one;

> And I next acknowledge duly
> Manhood taken by the Son
>
> And I trust and hope most fully
> In that manhood crucified . . .

Newman was not saying that the eternal Son of God became a male merely for males, but that the Son of God became incarnate as a human being. This is clear from his other popular hymn, 'Praise to the holiest in the height', of which one verse is:

> O generous love! that he, who smote
> in Man for man the foe,
> The double agony in Man
> for man should undergo.

The fact is that it is neither possible nor desirable to put an absolute veto on the use of either 'man' or 'manhood' in either liturgy or hymns. In fact we can say also the same of biblical translation. Is there a satisfactory alternative to 'Son of man' for the favoured expression of Jesus, *huios tou anthropou* (see Mark 2:10, 28; 8:31, 38)?

There is one last point we would like to make before we move on to look at the suggestions of extra canticles to be used in the liturgy. There is an intimate connection between the use of language and women's status and rights in the Church of God. However we need to consider that what is presently being proposed (and experimentally used in some places) may well turn out to be a case of merely treating the symptoms of a disease rather than the disease itself. Perhaps what is more urgently needed than changes in language is an exposition of the Christian doctrine of the equality of the sexes before God, and of their essential, God-ordained complementarity. If we can think through this doctrine then we shall be better placed to see where there is need for revision of language.

New canticles for use with the ASB

The Liturgical Commission tells us that the ASB allows freedom in the choice of canticles at certain points, and then,
on this basis, provides four new canticles. The first is Isaiah
66:10–14a,18b; the second an adaptation of St Anselm's 'Prayer
to St Paul'; the third, Wisdom 10:15–19, 20b–21; and the fourth
Ecclesiasticus 51:13–18a, 20b–22. They are chosen because of
their use of the words 'mother' and 'she' for the deity.

We cannot object in principle to the use of texts from either
the Old Testament (one canticle) or the Apocrypha (two texts).
And we have such a high opinion of the theology and spirituality of St Anselm of Canterbury that we do not wish to object
to texts by him being used in the English Church. What we
feel needs to be said with respect to these canticles is the
following:

1 If used without explanation, the text from Isaiah 66 could
   be seen as justifying the use of Mother in addressing the
   Lord God. The text uses a simile only, not a fully developed
   metaphor, and this point needs to be remembered. 'As a
   mother comforts her child so will I comfort you' is a long
   way from saying God is our Mother and we are her children.
2 The texts from the Apocrypha provide examples of the
   personification of divine wisdom. Both the Hebrew
   (*Hokmah*) and the Greek (*Sophia*) words for wisdom are
   in the feminine gender. So the pronoun 'she' occurs in these
   canticles as a substitute for 'wisdom'. 'She has been the
   delight of my heart' and 'She was their shelter by day and
   a blaze of stars by night' are not references to Yahweh. They
   are examples of the personification of the divine attribute of
   wisdom. To assume that these female gender words and the
   female pronoun refer to an actual female divine being is as
   dangerous an extrapolation as to say that abstract nouns in
   the masculine gender refer to sexual males. This may seem
   obvious, but it is the case that much has been made in
   the USA by feminist theologians of the personification of

wisdom and the fact of its feminine gender. One such
repeated sentence has been: 'Divine Sophia is Israel's God
in the language and Gestalt of the Goddess.'

3 The canticle based on St Anselm's 'Prayer to St Paul'
begins:

> Jesus, as a mother you gather your people to you:
> you are gentle with us as a mother with her children.

(For the full text see *The Prayers and Meditations of St
Anselm*, tr. Benedicta Ward, Penguin, 1973, pp. 141ff.)
Again we wish to comment that we have here only a simile
and not a developed metaphor. Anselm calls Jesus a mother
because he gave birth to the new Israel (the Church)
through his sufferings and death, just as a mother gives
birth to her child through the pains of labour (often causing
death in medieval times).

After Anselm, the theme of Christ our mother was taken up
by Cistercian groups. Jesus' 'motherhood' was used to highlight
both the painful 'labour' of Christ in his passion/death giving
birth to the new age/new creation, and the constant loving care
and nursing and feeding of his 'little ones' – the people of the
new age – by him. (The evidence is well presented by Caroline
W. Bynum in her study, *Jesus as Mother: studies in the spirituality of the high Middle Ages* [1982].)

Today it is Julian of Norwich who is perceived by many
people as both justifying and encouraging this medieval description of Jesus the Saviour. Further, since she refers to 'God
our Mother', she is seen by some people as justifying and
encouraging talk of the motherhood of God. Certainly she
speaks of Christ as mother because of his 'labour pains' and
'nurturing milk', and she relates the former to the 'sacrament
of the altar' and the latter to the Church as the 'mother of all
the faithful' (see her *Revelations of Divine Love*, chs 58–62).
We must ask what she meant when she wrote: 'God is as truly
our Mother as he is our Father' (ch. 59). In the context she is
speaking of the eternal God as a Trinity of Persons, and, since

the second Person became incarnate as Jesus, whom she calls
Mother, then 'God is truly our Mother'. She means the Word
incarnate, the son with human flesh as Messiah, for here God
in our human nature is as a mother to us in his work as Saviour.
However she has no intention of changing the biblical naming
of God as Father, Son and Holy Spirit. She seeks to convey
only the saving work of the Son in his human flesh through the
image of a mother. It may seem odd to us, but what is odd
now was not necessarily odd in medieval times.

The biblical basis for such talk from Anselm and Julian is
not difficult to find. Jesus yearned to gather the people of
Jerusalem under his saving grace as a hen gathers her chicks
under her wings (Matt. 23:27; Luke 13:34). St Paul told the
churches that his pains in bringing them into existence through
conversion and sanctification were like those of a woman in
childbirth (Gal. 4:19) and his care for them was like a mother
caring for her children (1 Thess. 2:7).

Conclusion

We wish to separate various related but different problems –
the problem of sexist language with respect to human beings
from the problem of sexist language with respect to God. We
are willing to go a way on the road of inclusive language in
liturgy when the reference is to human beings – provided it did
not concede larger principles and did not offend more people
than it helped. But, as we shall indicate in the next chapter,
we are opposed to inclusive language being used of deity.
Further we want to separate the problem of the true and right
appreciation of women as equal with men before God our
Creator and Redeemer, from the problem of adopting inclusive
language in liturgy. We believe that there needs to be a clearer
and bolder exposition of the Christian doctrines of the God-
ordained complementarity of women and men.

7

Inclusive Language for God

When we speak of feminism in the Church we need to bear in mind that it is a movement/ideology existing in a variety of expressions. To try to understand this variety we shall first describe what we may call the two wings of the movement or the two ends of the spectrum of feminism. Then we shall look at examples of changes in ways of addressing God advocated by those in what we may call the middle ground of feminism.

The two wings

There are women whom we may call Christian feminists who are Christians first and feminists second. That is, they seek to incorporate their feminist insights and principles into their essentially otherwise conservative Christianity (which may be of a Catholic, Evangelical or Charismatic variety). An example from England is Elaine Storkey, a frequent broadcaster and author of *What's Right with Feminism* (SPCK, 1985).

They accept the basic authority of the Holy Scriptures for faith and morals, insist that both men and women are made in the image, after the likeness of God, and that both sexes ought to be given equal dignity, and treated with equal respect in the Church. They press for inclusive, or non-exclusive, language of human beings in Church services and want to see more references to God which present the Godhead through feminine/motherly similes.

The booklet *Making Women Visible*, to which we referred in Chapter 6, may be said in general terms to have accepted their views, which, of course, are shared by a lot of educated men. We ourselves also share many of their concerns and have much respect for them.

At the other end of the spectrum, and on the opposite wing of the movement, are those who are feminists first and Christians second. They intend that Christianity should fit into their vision of feminism, and where it cannot fit it should be discarded. Though we have seen ten or more American publications which espouse, explain and commend this form of feminism, we find the clearest, most succinct statement of this position to be written by an academic teaching in Scotland: Daphne Hampson ('The challenge of feminism to Christianity', *Theology*, vol. lxxxviii, no. 725, September 1985). She explains that 'feminists are striving for women equally to be able to conceive of themselves as first class citizens, as those who organize the world. They believe that women should not have to find their identity in relation to men to a greater extent than do men in relation to women.' This outlook, she believes, represents a basic challenge to traditional Christianity, which has come out of a patriarchal context. For all those central to Judaism and Christianity have been men – from Abraham to Isaiah to Jesus to Paul. Women were related to them merely as wives, mothers, sisters and companions. She proceeds to identify the real problem in these words.

Christianity is a religion which has a historical referent. It is not an a priori religion founded on human religious experience, or on reason. It is grounded in particular historical events and finds expression in concrete symbolism. However, that very particularity, that very concretion, is sexist. Christianity cannot shed that sexism so long as it retains, as it must, the historical referent. Moreover, the historical referent serves to reinforce the sexism in the present; for it is not as though that history, those parables and that person of Christ are just any history, stories and person. They are normative. They form a model of what God is like and how we should relate to one another.

We agree! However we would not want to use the words sexist and sexism.

So it is not surprising that there is a measure of agreement between a conservative Christian like C. S. Lewis (in his essay 'Priestesses in the Church') and a genuine feminist of the 1980s. They join hands in agreeing that Christianity is tied to a system in which God is addressed through male symbolism. However the implication for the feminist is different from that of Lewis. While he opposed both the ordination of women and the addressing of God as Mother, the feminist feels obliged to create a new religion – a new form of Christianity perhaps – which is not sexist. She wants a new religion in which she is treated in all ways as the equal of a male person, and this means saying goodbye to traditional Christianity.

So we see that one form of feminism may be accommodated by traditional Christianity, but another cannot be (in fact does not wish to be) so accommodated. The genuine, full-blooded feminist sees her feminist principles as fundamental: the Christian feminist sees her feminist principles as – in some way – subject to the call and criteria of Jesus Christ.

The middle ground

Between the two ends of the spectrum of religious/Christian feminism are those feminists (with their male supporters) who believe that genuine Christianity and authentic feminism can be married if each side is prepared to make accommodations. On the one hand the feminists are prepared to stay within the Church and on the other, in return, ask only for equal treatment (not special treatment which is their right because of long discrimination against them). That is, they want the way of ordination to all orders of ministry opened to them; and they insist that inclusive language be used both of human beings and of God in all services of worship.

Here, we may point out, there arises an erroneous view of priesthood which has come to be accepted by many, that the priest represents humanity before God. The argument runs that, because of this representational role, women as well as men ought to be included in the priesthood – otherwise the female part of humanity is disenfranchised before God. However it is Jesus Christ alone, in the relation of his humanity to his divinity – his creaturely nature as man in relation to his uncreated nature as the eternal Word by whom all things were made – who represents and remakes/recapitulates all humanity in himself. The taking of our manhood into God enables both male and female to be redeemed. It is the function of the priest to point to Christ in symbolism and imagery appropriate to the mode of the incarnation, not himself (or herself) to represent mankind before God. This 'representative' role is not found in the Ordinal (the book of ordination services of the Church of England). Moreover this call for an all-embracing priesthood – male and female – can only disparage, or even cast away, the highest vocation and dignity ever accorded to a human being – Mary in her womanhood called to bear God.

In the American Episcopal Church (as in other denominations in North America) feminists and their supporters have achieved some of their objectives. It is well known that women are being ordained to the priesthood and that one has been consecrated a bishop. Further, trial/experimental services using inclusive language for humans and God are being widely used and approved by many bishops. It is common to hear God addressed as Mother in parish services. A similar state of affairs is developing in the New Zealand Anglican Church; and we are familiar in England with small groups who seek publicity for their feminist or inclusive language liturgies.

What the feminists of the middle ground do not appear sufficiently to take into account is that the whole concept of inclusive language is itself a culturally-conditioned product of post-Second World War society. For if, as they insist, the whole biblical teaching about God is conditioned and warped by the ancient practice of patriarchy, then the same type of argument can be used against their own position. In fact all ideologies are culturally conditioned – some more obviously than others – and western feminism is no exception.

What we are seeking to present is the view that God in self-revelation is not and in fact cannot be culturally conditioned, even though we in our reception can be (but need not be). Certainly Israelite patriarchy was culturally conditioned and any view of God developed from that model was/is so also. But the God who reveals himself and who has taught us how to receive his revelation is not to be equated with a supernatural form of a Jewish patriarch/Father. He is to be heard, seen, worshipped, trusted, loved and obeyed on his own terms.

From motherly description to motherly address

We have already noted that there is a strand of the Old Testament in which God is described in motherly terms (see ch. 3). The question raised by the feminist movement is whether we have a right to move from describing God as motherly to addressing God as Mother.

The position we have adopted is that the distinction between description and address is important, and must not be blurred. Approaching the God who is holy love is a unique experience given to us in the act of worship and prayer, when we encounter God because he has first encountered us. To name and call upon God is awesome; and it is not a right but a privilege granted by God in grace and mercy. This being so, in our approach to this God we ought only to use these names and forms of address which he has revealed to us and authorised in his self-naming in Jesus. Since Holy Scripture, which is the witness to divine revelation, provides no precedent or authorisation for addressing God as Mother, we are not free to do so, even if we felt that we could do so in an appropriate and orthodox way. We must address God as 'the Father of our Lord Jesus Christ'.

However, having made our position clear, we wish also to say that we can understand how some who, with us, accept the

authority of sacred Scripture, still feel that to address God
reverently on occasions as 'our Mother in heaven' is admissible
– indeed desirable. These Christian feminists feel that the distinction between description and address ought not to be
pressed, for they see a natural movement of the human mind
from reading/hearing descriptions of God's motherly care to
addressing God as Mother. Also they point out that since God
is addressed in the Old Testament via the imagery of lifeless
objects (such as Rock, Fortress and Shield) they cannot see
how using a metaphor based upon a female human being, who
is made in God's image and after his likeness, can be anything
but helpful in certain circumstances. What can be harmful, they
argue, in developing a simile into a metaphor/symbol?

In the first instance this is to beg the question of the image
of God. We note that it is humanity that is made in the image
and after the likeness of God – that is, humanity in the unity
of its diversity, male and female bound in mutual respect and
love. It is not the male without the female or the female without
the male which is the image. We refer to what has already been
said on this subject and on the related matter of the significance
of 'person' in the light of the doctrine of the Trinity. In the
second place there is all the difference in the world between
the proper phrase 'made in the image of God', and its loose
and incorrect usage 'made as the image of God'. There is, as
has been noted already, only one image of God, and that is
Jesus Christ, who is the image of what he actually is. He is
both the reality of God and the image of God. It is only in
Jesus that humanity finds its dignity and vocation as the creature made in the image of God. This attitude to female symbolism being transferred to a description of God is done behind
the back of Christ, as it were, and is a human attempt to
better the revelation and reconciliation fulfilled in him. It is an
improper and unwarranted use of imagery.

Our response to this question is to emphasise that to accept
revelation and reconciliation as that in and by which God has
mastered and transformed the environment (see ch. 1) is also
to accept that God has revealed to us who he is and how we

are to come to him and address him. We are the creatures: God is the Creator. We stand in need of forgiveness and reconciliation; God is the God of mercy and of grace. We lack words by which to speak to God; God has given us words to use as we accept his invitation to draw near to him. We must use what he has graciously given us, and be grateful to God for giving us both the words to speak to him and the way into his presence, in Christ Jesus, the Word made flesh.

But is there a genuine compromise possible through the occasional use of the expression, 'O God, our motherly Father'? We have recognised that God as Father lacks any gender, and in the Word made flesh exercised mastery through vulnerability and tenderness. Here the strength of God is indeed the weakness of men. We would say also that God embraces, while also totally transcending, the distinctive human ways of being persons and parents. 'Personhood' is dependent upon God, who is beyond all created being but creates in love. God is not dependent on human personhood. Therefore if we are seeking to set aside any view of God which suggests maleness or patriarchy or 'crude sovereignty, lordship, power', we can see it may be helpful in discussion to use such a phrase as 'motherly Father'; but we cannot see how it adds to the addressing of God, if Christians are taught the content of God's self-revelation from Scripture. In fact we believe it would be confusing and unsettling for many worshippers if introduced into the Lord's Prayer or other public prayers.

Perhaps the strongest argument for including 'mother' language in the addressing of God is at the psychological level. It is well known that many a mother acts towards her children as if she were both mother and father. This is due to the absence of the father or to his lack of involvement. Children in such circumstances may well find it difficult to respond to 'father language' in religion. However our point is that all of us, whether we have a good relationship with our fathers or not, need to learn about 'God our Father' by being taught from sacred Scripture. Not even the best possible relation with a human father is sufficient to supply the content of the symbol of 'our Father'. The most we can claim is that it is easier for a person with a healthy view of fatherhood to begin to appreciate, through the inspiration of the Holy Spirit, that this fatherhood points beyond itself to that which gives it being and meaning and value, to the 'God and Father of our Lord Jesus Christ', who cannot be adequately addressed or described by any, or all, human terms. For the knowing of God as Father is first and foremost a spiritual relationship of faith and love brought about by the secret operation of the Holy Spirit in the act we call regeneration.

By now we have made it clear where we stand and what we think is right and appropriate in our ways of addressing God. But to reinforce our point we wish now to examine what is involved in the actual addressing of God as Mother in a regular and consistent way. We do this because we suspect that many who do so have not considered the implications for theology and spirituality of this form of address.*

A theology of motherhood?

Let us consider what is involved if Christians are to begin to address God as Mother and to treat this metaphor as a strict equivalent in a complementary way to that of Father. What will this new metaphor/symbol tell us about God? We have seen that 'Father' gains its content and power through its use by Jesus against the background of the Old Testament. From where does 'Mother' gain its content and power? The simile of motherhood with respect to God is based, in the Bible, on human experience and observation.

* Our concern has been with the Godhead and his self-revelation. By that revelation we are taught that there is a supernatural, spiritual reality, a fallen angel, called the Devil or Satan. This opponent of Christ and his Church is presented to us in Scripture through male symbolism and gender. However we know that angels, good or bad, are without sexual distinctions. Thus by their own logic those who wish to call God 'Mother and Father' ought also to refer to Satan via both masculine and feminine symbolism and pronouns. However we are not conscious that they are doing so.

The mother conceives, bears in the womb, gives birth, suckles, nurtures, cares for, is patient with and educates her child. She is the model of kindness, tenderness and sensitivity. However if 'Mother' is to become an address for God, then it has to transcend sexual connotation and function asexually so that it does not suggest in the slightest way that God is female. If it does suggest that, then this is an unwarranted and even heretical projection, on the same pattern as Gnosticism or Arianism, of human images into the eternal being of God. But how can the word take on such a role unless someone with equal influence, attraction, significance and authority as Jesus Christ takes it up and uses it as her/his special or unique way of addressing God? If there were such a person and this were to occur, then from her/his example the content of 'Mother' would have an authentic reference built into it. To talk in this way is to begin to displace Jesus Christ as the only mediator between God and humankind, and to put alongside him another who claims to be the way, truth and life. It is the first step into heresy. We acknowledge only One, the Word made flesh, who is the way, truth and life, and we deny the false claims of other authorities, however attractive their cultural expressions, to intrude, add to or even displace this One.

Possibly the call for the use of Mother is related to a mistaken view as to what the Christian tradition has affirmed concerning God. If the call is intended to go alongside Father in order to declare that God is not a male deity, then we understand the point but deny its appropriateness. This is not the way to counteract a heresy; it is only to compound that heresy. For it is heretical if anyone thinks that 'Father' projects male sexuality into the eternal being of God.

Possibly the call for the use of Mother is related to the real fact of discrimination against women, and it represents a protesting word to heaven which could be expanded to say 'It is not men alone who are made in the image and after the likeness of God.' If this is so, then our response is to express sympathy, but to suggest also that the way to right wrongs on earth is not to change our address/words to heaven. The

granting of equal rights to women will certainly be helped by
the offering of efficacious prayers to God; however there is no
need to modify/reject the biblical witness to offer that prayer.
It is surely better to pray to the Father through the Son in the
power of the Holy Spirit, for we are promised a reply to such
prayer.

Now we come to our final point. If feminists and/or their
supporters insist on including an address to God as Mother in
the public prayers – especially the Eucharistic Prayer – of the
Church, then we fear that the doctrine of the Holy Trinity will
be eclipsed, even denied. And, as we shall show, the Trinity
is the greatest, and indeed the only, hope for men and women
in true humanity, for by this doctrine revealed by God as God,
we learn that God is a community of holy love.

The doctrine/dogma of the Holy Trinity may seem rather
remote and difficult to understand when expressed in the precise and involved terminology of the *Quicunque Vult* (the so-
called Athanasian Creed). Such precision was necessary (and
remains necessary) to guard against erroneous statement and
careless teaching. If we are wrong here, then we are wrong
everywhere. The proclamation that God, who is one God,
exists eternally as a community of Persons (Father, Son and
Holy Spirit), is the very foundation of everything we call Christian. The mutual interpenetration of the Persons in infinite,
eternal and holy love, brings into being yet transcends all
human (female and male) love; and from this creative Trinity
there goes forth that same love which created us in the beginning to reconcile, save and redeem us. Here is the very opposite
of all pictures of the Godhead as being the source of male
domination and of making only males in the divine image and
after God's likeness – which, of course, is a travesty of the
orthodox Christian tradition, but a travesty which has been
sometimes wrongly perpetuated. We want to say that only the
orthodox teaching of 'God-in-relationship' can undermine false
views of male-dominated Church life, and provide us with an
enriching and liberating understanding of what it means for all
human beings to be made in the image and after the likeness

of God, and for males and females to be complementary in God's care and grace.

Also we want to say that those who are pressing for the inclusion of Mother alongside or instead of Father are (whether they know it or not) not only distorting the doctrine that God is a Trinity of love, but they are also causing its abandonment. The revealed content of this doctrine is so finely balanced that to interfere with it in any major way is to cause a change in doctrine. This is clearly seen by the radical feminists, and so they abandon Christianity. In fact any tampering with the doctrine of the Trinity leads to either unitarianism or polytheism.

All who participate in liturgical worship are familiar with the *Gloria Patri*, 'Glory to the Father and to the Son and to the Holy Spirit, as it was in the beginning, is now and ever shall be, world without end, Amen.' This is a doxological expression of Trinitarian faith, using the generally accepted names for the three Persons of the one God. The use of these three names together, and not any other possible combination of names for God, came about after much debate and controversy in the patristic period. The Church of the East and the West came to see that the three names together were the appropriate and right way of confessing the Trinity in unity.

An alternative to the *Gloria Patri* has been advocated and put to trial use in the American Episcopal Church recently. This does not include the terms 'Father' and 'Son', for it is an attempt to eliminate sexist language from the way we address God. It is: 'Honor and glory to God, and to the eternal Word and to the Holy Spirit: God the One in Three, for ever and ever, Amen.' The revisers tell us that it is intended to preserve the orthodox doctrine of the Trinity and that it is preferable to doxologies which refer to God as 'Creator, Redeemer and Sustainer/Sanctifier'. (The lady assistant bishop of Massachusetts used the latter doxology before beginning her sermon at her consecration on 11 February 1989.)

But does this new Gloria set forth the praise of God as a Trinity of Persons? Has the determined attempt to remove the sexist associations allegedly connected to Father and Son had the unintended result of distorting the orthodox, classic doctrine of the Trinity? It certainly contains the seeds of confusion: 'God' is used both of the first Person of the Trinity and of the Trinity itself. Thus it is possible to take the 'eternal Word' and 'Holy Spirit' as inferior Persons or modes of being not included within the Godhead/deity here named God. So the phrase 'honor and glory' is both ascribed to God who is defined later as 'One in Three' and to 'the eternal Word and the Holy Spirit'; and there is no necessary, built-in connection in this formula to identify the 'eternal Word and the Holy Spirit' as two Persons. However, even if we discount the problem of using the same name for the Godhead as for the first Person, the problem remains as to why in the new Gloria a relatively little-used title for the second Person is used instead of the title and name hallowed by constant use in both Scripture and tradition.

Even to replace constantly the familiar 'Father, Son and Holy Spirit' with 'Almighty God, Creator, Redeemer and Sustainer' has the twofold effect of first, wrenching apart the being of God from the acts of God (and God is as he acts and acts as he is), and secondly of changing the doctrine of the Trinity as a Trinity of Persons to a trinity of expressions of the one Person of God. This is the old heresy of what is called modalism or merely economic trinitarianism wherein God is conceived as one God and one mode of being, who expresses himself in three ways rather than existing as three Persons. The fact is that only the God who is truly and really a Trinity can be love without any creature being involved. If God is a Trinity of Persons, then God is love eternally existing as a community of love. Only in this latter doctrine is there real hope and salvation for us all.

It would appear that the determination to serve a modern cultural phenomenon brings the possibility of confusion into the central doctrine of Christianity. The sad truth is that this determination and desire is so overwhelming that it dismisses the lessons so carefully, reverentially and sacrificially learnt in the tradition of the Church. In fact such revision ought to serve as a modern cautionary tale to all who want to improve upon the classic statements of Trinitarian faith.

Epilogue

This work has been undertaken within the context of the demands of parochial/diocesan responsibilities. It has not been produced leisurely, removed from the heat of the day or from the joy and privilege of dealing with pastoral circumstances of men and women and children, and the practicalities of working out the gospel which these involve. Whatever shortcomings are apparent, we hope it will be realised that time has had to be made to write this in the midst of other responsibilities.

We are also aware that it may appear that we are largely negative in attacking a particular trend. But we have tried to be positive in asserting the principles of the Catholic and Evangelical faith which speaks of the mystery of the Word made flesh and the great positive truths of God and (in that light) of humanity. To underline this desire to be positive, we append the following statements.

We believe, teach and confess that:

1   What God eternally is in himself, he is towards us in Jesus Christ. For Jesus Christ is God speaking and acting in our flesh and nature for us and for our salvation. As such he is both the sufficient revelation of God and our complete reconciliation with God.
2   Jesus Christ is the essential content and truth of Holy Scripture, the words of which Scripture both point beyond themselves as the unique witness to him, and serve as the record of revelation.
3   The essential content of Holy Scripture is summed up in the historic creeds. The Church in continual faithfulness

to Jesus Christ must set forth with one mind and one mouth what the Lord conferred, the apostles proclaimed in the gospel and the fathers safeguarded in the creeds.

4 There is no other authority, truth or insight which may be placed alongside Scripture and this credal tradition in their relation of faithfulness to Jesus Christ, as an addition to them, or be elevated as a substitute for them. Therefore the role of reason is, in faithfulness to that Jesus Christ, to proclaim him who is truth at every time and place, from the vantage point of this truth disclosed, to the continual edification of the Church and the conversion of the world.

5 The form of this proclamation is, as Scripture gives us and the tradition teaches us, by use of terms and language appropriate to the nature of this truth, for this truth is both the way God addresses us and the way we may respond to God. We are called to listen to Christ the Truth, in reverence and obedience, and to be clothed with his gospel, rather than dressing him in our philosophies.

6 The terms so used to express the being of God as the Trinity in unity and the unity in Trinity (the one God existing as Father and Son bound in the bond of eternal love, the Holy Spirit) are beyond the human-centred content signified by the like terms of father and son and love applied to describe human experience and circumstances. Terms on the created, human level, when applied to God the Uncreated, are not to convey their earthly content into that eternal being of God.

7 That these terms therefore must be used with reverence and care, because they do not convey the divisions of human sexuality into God. They are commissioned by Jesus Christ himself for our proper use. To construe them as insufficient or defective by adding further terms from human sexuality such as 'mother', 'daughter', 'parent', is either a gross misunderstanding of their use or a deliberate attempt to subvert the way and grace of God in revelation and reconciliation, by deeming it to be lacking or defective.

8 Humankind is made in the image and after the likeness of

this God. It reflects, in its creaturely dimension of the complementarity of male and female in the one bond of human integrity, the unity of the Triune existence of the eternal God. As the Father is not the Son, nor the Son the Father, and as the Father does not exist without the Son or the Son without the Father, so too, there is neither self-sufficient male nor self-sufficient female. As the unity of the Godhead is a unity of the Holy Spirit, so the unity of humankind is found in the mutual respect of male and female in the richness and diversity of its existence.

9   This image of God is properly only Jesus Christ himself, who is what he images. In Christ we find the true existence and identity of humanity made in the image of God.

10 The human nature of Jesus Christ, the Word made flesh, is all-embracing, establishing the true identity, nature and bond of male and female before God in their unity and diversity. It is not a mechanical means of falsely confusing and merging human identity, but rather an establishing of true humanity – God's humanity.

11 The 'male' symbols/metaphors for God have been misused and misunderstood by men in the Church to support male domination. Therefore there is need for repentance and a new mind in this regard, for such errors can only lead to a travesty of Christianity and eventual heresy.

12 There is need for repentance and a new mind before the truth of Jesus Christ by those women and men who deliberately and wholeheartedly insist on addressing God as Mother and calling on others to do so. They are both rejecting God's revelation and rebelling against him by intruding into the eternal certain ideals and images drawn from a basis in cultural authority which is part of this passing world. To project their content into God is an alien and inappropriate use of images, and can only lead to heresy and the eventual rejection of Christianity.

Glory be to the Father and to the Son and to the Holy Spirit, three Persons, consubstantial, co-eternal, one God, now and throughout all ages. Amen.

DATE DUE			
MAY 22 1997			
			Printed in USA